Permission to Write

HOW TO WRITE A BOOK AND OTHER MYTHS FROM THE REAL
WORLD OF WRITING AND PUBLISHING

PATRICIA J. PARSONS

MOONLIGHT PRESS | TORONTO

PERMISSION TO WRITE: HOW TO WRITE A BOOK AND OTHER MYTHS FROM THE REAL WORLD OF WRITING AND PUBLISHING

Copyright © Patricia J. Parsons 2019

ISBN 978-0-9958882-2-7

ALL RIGHTS RESERVED. No part of this publication may be reproduced, distributed, or transmitted in any form or by any means, including photocopying, recording, or other electronic or mechanical methods, without the prior written permission of the publisher, except in the case of brief quotations embodied in critical reviews and certain other non-commercial uses permitted by copyright law. For permission requests, write to the publisher, addressed as follows:

moonlightpressinfo@gmail.com

Although the author and publisher have made every effort to ensure that the information in this book was correct at the time of publication, the author and publisher do not assume and hereby disclaim any liability to any party for any loss, damage, or disruption caused by errors or omissions, whether such errors or omissions result from negligence, accident, or any other cause.

Contents

Ode to the Unknown Writer 1
Writing that First Book: Tales from the Trenches 7
Becoming a Writer 19
In the Beginning was the Idea 27
You are What you Write 35
Cross-training for Writers 45
Reading, Writing and Keeping Journals 50
Ideas for Your Writing Practice 58
Deadlines, Schedules and Momentum, Oh My! 63
Other People: Is There Safety in Numbers? 74
Don't Publish Everything You Write: 84
A Glossary for the 21st Century Writer 91
Publishing Trends: Finding the Right Fit for You 101
The Publishing Process: Traditional Publishing 109
The Publishing Process: Self-publishing 117
Book Promotion 101: Who Will Read Your Book? 131
The Alphabet Soup of Book Marketing 139
Your Primary Promotional Tool: Your Book Cover 145
Traditional Tools for Book Promotion 154
The New Wave of Promotional Tools 171
Permission to write: Your Future 186
About the Author 197
Annotated list of my book-length publications 198
Sources 205

The Nature of a Myth

THIS BOOK EXPLORES THE INTERSECTION OF MYTHS AND REALITIES. It's about the fictitious and the real. It's about the difference between how you'd like it to be and how it is.

A myth is a story that may or may not have some basis in reality. By definition, a myth represents a popularly held belief that is largely unfounded or false. Note: Although it may have some basis in reality and offer some guidance, it doesn't tell the whole story of how it really is.

The reason I even mention this is because of the tsunami of books these days with titles like "Ten Sure-fire Ways to Make a Million Dollars with Your First Book" and other such lies. There are no ten sure-fire ways to make a million dollars with any book, your first or last. There isn't even one *sure-fire* way. It could happen, but no one can give you the magic bullet. It doesn't exist. There are no guarantees in life, and writing is perhaps among the least certain parts of life.

Although it is undoubtedly true that you could learn a lot from a step-by-step guide to writing a book (and if you search for "how to write a book" on a site like Amazon, you'll get over 20,000 hits), there is so much more involved. There are such mundane things as coming up with a brilliant idea and garnering the self-discipline to complete a manuscript – not to mention the myriad issues involved in getting that brilliant tome into the hands of readers eventually. But never mind those little details. Further, if you are looking for another co-dependent writer-friend to tell you that your work is brilliant and just keep writing, stop reading immediately. I am not that friend.

I refuse to tell other writers that their work is brilliant or even good when it is riddled with grammatical errors and usage problems. Or if the story makes no sense. And I will most certainly not tell an aspiring writer that his or her writing is good if it is boring. In my opinion, the most important thing a writer must do in his or her published work is ***never to bore the reader.***

I will also not tell an aspiring writer that there is a high degree of likelihood for success in the writing world. That is a bald-faced lie. It is beyond even a myth. There are certainly success stories – and you may yet be one of them – but for every successful writer, there are hundreds of thousands (perhaps millions in these days of self-publishing) who are not successful for a wide variety of reasons. But if you truly are a writer just waiting to emerge, then you'll appreciate a dose of reality among the myths you've been fed. I'm here to help you.

How to write a book? The very thought that there is "a way" to write a book is a myth. There are myriad ways. The best one for you will be your own.

As British philosopher Bertrand Russel once said, *"There is something feeble and a little contemptible about a man who cannot face the perils of life without the help of comfortable myths."* If you can face the perils of the writing life without succumbing to the comfort of the myths, then I think you're already halfway there. Join me on this journey as we expose the myths together.

Reality Check #1

Talent is not Enough: Writing Takes Passion and Commitment

"I never desire to converse with a man who has written more than he has read." ~ Samuel Johnson

ONE

Ode to the Unknown Writer

"How vain it is to sit down to write when you have not stood up to live."
~ Henry David Thoreau

THE LATE AMERICAN COMIC BOOK WRITER Len Wein once said, "Writers write. Others talk about it." He also said, "*A writer writes. Period. No matter if someone is buying your work or not.*" I happen to be in complete agreement with him, so this is where we start. You aren't a writer if you don't write, and if you are a writer (and you know this because you *do* write), you don't write to readers; you just write. And if what you write resonates with readers, that's terrific. But you might be one of those would-be writers sharing the writing philosophy of a young man I once overheard at a restaurant who said, "I don't want to write. I just want to *have written*." And therein lies one of the problems with today's writing and publishing world. How do I know this? Because I've been part of it since my first book was published in 1988.

But you might be among those who write who cannot seem to get out of the camp of the unknown writer. You know who you are. You're the one who desperately wants to spend your days as a writer and then see your words in print, but you are just a bit afraid to tell anyone that you are "a writer." Maybe you've written a book or two, have a website, perhaps have even self-published and have Twitter and Instagram followers. You belong to Facebook groups for writers. You're the one who surfs over to the Amazon stats to read the bestseller list—and once again, find that your name is not there. You're the one seeking those ebooks that all seem to suggest that there are "ten sure-fire ways to have a bestseller" or "seven magic bullets to writing success." You may not have yet followed that advice, but you're considering it. You are not to be deterred. As long as there is breath in your body, you will write, and you will be published, and you will hope for readers to follow. You are an unknown writer. Welcome to the club. It's growing larger every day. I have a secret to share with you. Those who seem to be making a good living from their ebooks are among the minority. It could happen to you if you know what you're doing, but there is no magic bullet. What worked for one writer may or may not work for you.

I'd now like to introduce you to the real world of writing and publishing books.

Twenty years ago, in the late 1990s, publishing pundits began sounding the alarm about the changes already underway in book publishing. Those changes were directly related to the dawn of the digital age. And the entire landscape of writing and publishing has changed—even for writers who have worked for years with traditional publishers. Like me.

By the early twenty-first century, it was becoming increasingly apparent that digitization of the publishing processes would have far-reaching effects, most of which were believed to save time and money for both publishers and authors. In 1999, David Chereb was the director of research at the *eForecast Institute* in Mission Viejo, California. At that time, he estimated that electronic publication reduced the time from rough draft to final online product by 75%. Perhaps even more remarkable was the emergence of the notion that publishers, as traditional gatekeepers of the whole process, would no longer be required to play this role. Those were the days when the only way for authors to see their books in print—and they were all "in print" at that time—was to submit oneself to the long, drawn-out, often soul-sucking cycle of submission-rejection-submission to agents and publishers, or to "vanity publish." Authors took the latter approach at their peril, recognizing the threat to both personal pocketbooks and reputation. There was not even the faintest likelihood that the book would ever find a reader with so-called vanity publishing. There were virtually no distribution channels open to the vanity-published author other than selling books out of the trunk of the author's car. Fast forward to 2019 and beyond, where everyone can be published—and quality be damned.

The data on the number of books published fluctuates depending on your source, but the number is increasing at a speed that boggles the mind, even of the most open-minded and creative among us. Bowker (the company that assigns ISBNs in the US—International Book Standard Numbers) keeps statistics on published books. In late 2018, they reported that self-publishing alone grew at a rate of more than 28% from the previous year, with over a million self-published books hitting distribution channels that year in addition to the traditionally published ones.

With millions of books published by every manner of publisher—big traditional, small traditional, small independents, self-publishers and every combination thereof—every year, you might think that people are buying and reading more than ever. You'd be wrong—sort of. In 2018, *New Yorker* writer Caleb Crain revisited a story he had written a decade earlier, at which time he had suggested that reading was in decline. This time around, it seemed even more evident. Americans, at least, read less than they used to.

According to Adam Rowe, writing in *Forbes* online, "88% of 2014 respondents told *BookNet* they had read a book in the last year, compared to just 81% in the 2018 survey, with a slow but steady decline (84%, 83%, and 82% across 2015, 2016, and 2017 respectively) in between." In Canada, the figures suggest that the number of people reading is declining gradually, but the number of books individual readers read seems to be increasing. So, the overall number of readers is declining in the face of increasing numbers of published books. However, each individual reader consumes more books. Can an individual reader make up for declining overall numbers of readers by simply reading more books? Good question. The answer has interesting implications for writers who can develop a following and keep those readers hooked on multiple books. That is, if they understand the realities of today's publishing world.

Traditional book sales appear to be declining, but electronic book sales are increasing. Despite this, the latest statistics available at the time of this writing, perhaps surprisingly, indicate that print books still outsell electronic books by a considerable margin. Regardless of format, the exponential rise in the number of published books without a concomitant increase in the overall number of readers means fewer sales to go around. It's simple math.

As an unknown writer, you'd probably be delighted to know that people who buy a Kindle by Amazon e-reader (or download the app to another device), on average, purchased four times as many books from Amazon as they were likely to have done in the year before making the change to electronic reading. But before you jump to the conclusion that it's now a piece of cake to get your masterpiece in front of those readers with their Kindles, Kobos, and other e-reading devices, we need to put on the brakes and begin to get a real sense of the truth of writing and publishing.

When literary agent John Boswell published his depressing book *The Awful Truth About Publishing: Why They Always Reject Your Manuscript and What you Can do About It* in 1986 (I keep a copy on my bookshelf just to keep me grounded in reality), he talked about the awful truth that over half a million books had been published worldwide in the decade from the mid-1970s to the mid-1980s. Only half a million? What were the unknown writers doing then? Sitting on their thumbs? Perhaps not. Here's what he said at the time:

> *"...as encouraging to aspiring authors as these numbers may at first seem, they are actually quite deceptive. For the truth is that the vast majority of people who dream of getting published never even come close."*

That was then. Unknown writers have always been writing. They just haven't been seeing their words in print. One more awful truth is that the digital age has made it much easier to have your book published—and much more difficult in so many ways. With millions of books published every year, it is truly disheartening to think that publishing your book is so easy, but ensuring its quality, then getting someone to read your book, now that is truly problematic.

John Boswell's book taught me one fundamental truth that has stayed with me throughout my writing career. He called it his awful truth #3: *You must sell a book three times*. It isn't enough to write a book and then simply expect it to be read. (If you are writing merely as catharsis, no one wants to read it anyway. Trust me on this. And if you are just writing for something to do in the evening—a hobby—don't worry about it. Publishing isn't on your radar.) If, however, you write so that others might learn from or be entertained by your work, *you need someone to read it*. For that to happen, at least in the old, pre-digital days, you had first to sell the book to a publisher, then to a bookstore owner and then to a reader. In some cases, four times, since many of the large, traditional publishing houses wouldn't then, and still won't, read your work unless you have an agent. So, you also have to sell it to an agent. (More about this merry-go-round in later chapters.) And in case you're unfamiliar with the wacky world of bookselling, print books are just about the only commodity that can still be sold on consignment. If a bookstore doesn't sell your book, it can return it to the publisher—the dreaded "returns." Oh, the world of publishing seemed so simple then.

These days, the awful truth is that even though we can short-circuit traditional book publishers by doing it ourselves, that still may not get the book into the reader's hands any more efficiently or even at all. For many writers, this is a recipe for publishing disaster or worse—financial calamity.

Not so long ago, I had the misfortune of ordering a self-published book from an online retailer. Unlike many traditional news sources and book reviewers, I have no fundamental objection to self-published books. What I do object to, however, is unedited self-published books that don't come with a warning label such as this: ***Warning! You are entering the pages of a book that will offend the stylistically, grammatically, and punctuation-obsessed among us!*** But alas, there was no such warning. The truth is that writers need editors if they expect anyone other than their families to read their work.

The Ten New 'Awful Truths' for the Unknown Writer

As the author of a dozen or so books (the majority of which were published by slogging through the traditional channels), I offer you the following awful truths about publishing in the twenty-first century.

Awful truth #1: The odds of achieving fame and fortune through your writing and publishing are a bit like your chances of winning the lottery. It could happen, but—well, you know the odds.

Awful truth #2: Finding a traditional publisher willing to publish your book does not predict a career as an accomplished writer. The publisher may never pick up another of your manuscripts.

Awful truth #3: Finding ideas for writing is easy; finding ideas that will resonate with publishers and readers can seem impossible.

Awful truth #4: You probably don't write as well as you think you do. (I learned this from William Zinsser, who said in his excellent book *On Writing Well*, "Few people know how poorly they write," and from editing student writers' work.)

Awful truth #5: Being part of a writing community can be a good thing or contribute to a developing co-dependency of mediocre writing.

Awful truth #6: The ease of self-publishing makes it simple to see your book in print or online, but it means that the competition is gruelling.

Awful truth #7: Make no mistake about it. Many, if not most, self-publishing companies are focused on selling products and services to writers. Without careful planning, you could end up in financial disaster.

Awful truth #8: Just because you have lots of Twitter and Instagram followers and friends on Facebook doesn't mean that they will buy your book.

Awful truth #9: Whether they are self-published or have been taken on by traditional publishers, authors must market and promote their own books.

Awful truth #10: Without a scorecard, it's challenging to figure out what's going on in the publishing world since every day seems to turn up a new model: self, vanity, co-op, traditional, indie, and the list goes on.

Writer Lillian Hellman is reported to have once said, *"They're fancy talkers...those writers. If I had to give young writers advice, I would say don't listen to writers talking about writing or themselves."* With apologies to Lillian, I plan to do both. If you're still with me, I invite you along on my adventures through the publishing world. Perhaps we can learn a thing or two together along the way.

TWO

Writing that First Book: Tales from the Trenches

"When I got my library card, that's when my life began."
~ Rita Mae Brown

I WAS, IF NOTHING ELSE, A NERD in my early years. When both my sisters took part-time, after-school jobs at a local grocery store, I marched into the local children's library and landed myself a job. For several years, I spent ten wonderful hours every week stacking books. Every other Saturday morning, it was my responsibility to set up the film projector for the children. Parents would bring their children and sit them in a circle on little chairs where they'd sit, enraptured by the film. Then it was storytime. Oh, the story! I was never senior enough to be the one to select the story, but I loved to read it. I was also the only one in my first-year university class who could thread a film into one of those old reel-to-reel projectors. And speaking of university—you can probably guess where I spent my part-time job hours.

I spent those happy hours among the stacks of thousands of books, pushing around my little metal cart laden with returns, reshelving according to the Library of Congress system (I had graduated from the Dewey Decimal System used at the children's library) and drinking in the smells and the quiet of the life of books. To say that books have always been important to me would be a gross understatement. In fact, I not only wanted to read them. I also wanted to write them when I was thirteen.

It was a delicious thought, that notion of writing a book. It was many years later before I did that very thing.

Everyone I know thinks that once you have your name on a book cover, you have it made, right? Fame? Fortune? I think not. And yet, there is something about seeing your name on that cover. It's a great feeling of accomplishment, but it's not fame, and it's certainly not fortune.

"Rich and famous and writing books are only linked when they're in that order." Or so said writer Jenny Diski back in 2007 in *The Guardian* book blog. This exhortation resonated with me then and still does. I especially sat up and took notice when, later in the article, she says: "Get a grip, people, either get on with it and write your book, at the weekend, after work, before work, during the vacation, or on a pitiful part-time income, or choose a proper way to get rich and famous." Presumably, that proper way has nothing to do with writing for a living. Somewhat depressing, don't you think? I've often said that books don't sell themselves unless your name is Oprah (or a reasonable facsimile). And yet we continue to write, and we continue to hope. Why?

There's a lot more to life than being rich, and if Andy Warhol was right, we all really do get that fifteen minutes of fame—but that's all most of us ever get. Just ask all those so-called reality TV stars. We still hope that the next book will strike a chord and take off. After all, writing a book is like opening your heart and mind to an audience and inviting them in. Sometimes they come in, and sometimes they don't. Despite all the times when they have not ventured into my books, I still have stories left to tell, and I'm going to tell them. You may feel the same way. As Jonathan Sacks said, *"Follow your passion. Nothing—not wealth, success, accolades or fame—is worth spending a lifetime doing things you don't enjoy."*

Fame, or something like it

What does it mean to be famous, especially for writers? It's an interesting question since many writers, even those whose books are on the bestseller list, are not exactly household names, suggesting limited fame at best. On any given morning, you can check the bestseller list in the *New York Times,* which is arguably the highest-profile of all the bestseller lists. Or you might go online to see the Amazon list.

How many of those writers' names do you recognize? Perhaps there's a Robert Galbraith, who is very famous if you know that he is J.K. Rowling's pen name when she's writing about private detective Cormoran Strike rather than Harry Potter. Perhaps you'll see someone like Michelle Obama, famous for something other than her writing—which is often the case. But it is more likely that you recognize very few of the names unless they are serial writers in a genre that you read regularly. Most writers are unknown to most people.

Marilyn Monroe once famously said, *"Fame doesn't fulfill you. It warms you a bit, but that warmth is temporary."* However fleeting these days, fame can be a kind of acknowledgement of achievement for some people. Writers, like everyone else, each have their own benchmarks for success. Fame is often one of them. You seemingly have made it if people know who you are because of your books. But unknown writers far outnumber well-known writers, and if you want to write that book, you may have to settle for the sense of accomplishment that comes with a job well done or, at the very least, completed. The fame you might think is a given as an author is more than likely going to be elusive. The case remains: first, you have to write the book.

The first book

You've probably heard it said more than once: *there's a book in everyone*. But for most people, that's where it stays (and make no mistake, from some readers' and publishers' perspectives, that is precisely where many of them ought to stay—inside the writer). Sometimes, though, for better or for worse, we need that book to come out.

There are those among us—and you may be one of them—who just have to get that book out and onto paper, or at least into a computer. Some of us just need to write. We need to write every day, and we need to write about all kinds of things that we see, hear about, read about, question and create in our mind's eye. Then the time finally arrives, sooner or later, that we just need to feel that finished book in our hands. At least, that's the way it was for me. So, just how did that happen the first time? How did I get to the point where a publisher said, "Yes"? Let me tell you a story.

My first book started way back in my early career. I worked as an "organ procurement officer" for a large multi-organ transplant program within a major hospital facility. Aside from the snickering often engendered by the term "organ procurement" proudly displayed on my business card (I was in my mid-twenties), it was a job fraught with responsibilities and ethical landmines.

My duties fell into two general areas. First, I was responsible for public communication programming designed to persuade people to sign their organ donor cards. Second, I taught health professionals how to ask the right question at the right time. I was also responsible for what is referred to as coordinating organ donation, the actual on-the-ground process by which organs are donated from brain-dead patients to desperate souls awaiting a new lease on life. Throughout my time in this position, I felt very acutely that there was a story to be told. So, I kept notes, an activity I highly recommend for any would-be author regardless of genre. Then, I started to research how to find an appropriate publisher for a book about organ donation ethics and politics.

A little common sense goes a long way for writers seeking publication. It was true then, and it continues to be true. Common sense told me that I had to be sure that I did not shop the book to publishers who had no interest in it and did not publish books in my genre or topic. Since then, I have found out that this kind of common sense doesn't seem to be all that common among writers these days—at least as far as traditional publishers are concerned. So, I knew that I could avoid all those who specialized in fiction, children's literature, fantasy, science fiction, etc. I was looking for a publisher who took on health-related, nonfiction trade books (a trade book is one for the general public rather than one for professionals). It occurred to me that if I tried to sell this idea to the wrong publisher, it would mark me as a rank amateur.

Figuring out which publishers would be appropriate was even more difficult back then. It was the late 1980s, so I didn't have the luxury of sitting at my desk with Google to search for publishers in health-related nonfiction, nor did I have Amazon to comb through for similar books and see who published them as I would do today. I had to go to a book store to see those similar books, and

I had to buy a copy of *Writer's Market*, the go-to compendium for all things publishing, which is still a valuable tool even today (it's updated every year).

After I figured out which publishers might be in the mix, I learned to write a query letter to precisely and eloquently inquire about their interest in my particular project. I thought a lot about what I wanted to accomplish with this particular book—its purpose. Then, I wrote down a paragraph describing this. This would be my *elevator pitch*, and it would be my calling card. Today, I'd probably call it my *blurb*. I knew I'd have to have an answer when someone inevitably asked me, "What's your book about?" And you will, too.

Then I did what every book/blog/seminar aimed at aspiring writers tells you not to do: I called a publisher on the telephone. I do not recommend this approach, especially today.

I was living on the east coast of Canada at the time, and I just happened to find myself in Toronto. One of the publishers on the list happened to be in Toronto. I happened to be stuck at Pearson International Airport in Toronto for a couple of idle hours, making a connection. There happened to be a bank of telephones right in front of me in the departure lounge (remember: it was the 1980s before we were all chained to our smartphones).

Although now a mere memory from my distant past, I can still recreate the feeling I had as I walked over to the phone, the telephone number on a small piece of paper clutched in my hand, then punched in the number. I can still feel my heartbeat surging as I listened to the sound of the phone ringing on the other end of the line. I think I almost hung up! When it was answered, I asked to speak with the editor I had identified (having a name is important, I had been told). I fully expected them to tell me that she was unavailable then or any other time. No one was as surprised as I was when she picked up. I knew that I had mere moments to make my pitch, so I gave her my short speech without stopping, then ended with the question, "Would you be interested in seeing a full proposal with a view to publishing?" She said, "Yes." Just like that.

That's when the work started. I had to learn how to prepare a book proposal.

And so, it begins

The moment the publisher said "yes," she was interested in seeing more about my book with a view to possible publication, it was the moment that I knew I'd have to learn to write a dynamite book proposal. I'd done enough research by then to know that I'd need to have that elevator pitch and a fully fleshed-out pitch in the form of a proposal to send before anyone would agree to publish my first nonfiction book. Now, I needed to learn the elements of a great book proposal, and I had to execute it—and fast—before she lost interest.

I've held tightly to a personal belief for many years: I believe that you can learn just about anything short of brain surgery from a well-crafted book. So, I immediately rushed out and bought anything I could find on the topic of writing book proposals. These days, all a would-be author has to do is visit one of the online mega-bookstores, search "How to write book proposals," and *voila*! Hundreds of books to choose from. And this doesn't even include all those blog posts that writers have shared on the topic. This is both a blessing and a curse because you now have a much more complicated job of figuring out which ones are the most useful, most trustworthy, and best-written. Trust me on this: they are not all great references. Back in the day, I had to go to a brick-and-mortar bookstore to examine the possibilities.

Over the years, I've learned a thing or two about book proposals to the point where a few years ago, another one of my publishers (who had also said "yes") suggested to me that I should teach other writers to write proposals since mine were so well-crafted—at least in his view. Of course, I was flattered, so I'm going to share my personal pointers that I have honed since that first proposal.

Book proposals are essential to nonfiction (and sometimes fiction) writers who want to be published by "traditional" publishers. What I mean by traditional publishers (which I'll delve into much more later) is those publishers who themselves take on the financial risks associated with publishing your book (they edit, design, market, etc.). In fact, they might even give you money upfront (an advance against royalties). If you want to publish it yourself, you don't actually need a proposal, but I'd recommend developing one for yourself anyway. For now, we're going the route of the traditional publisher, which is the route I've been taking with my nonfiction. This route requires you to understand that you have to sell your book three times—a situation that I've mentioned before and will again.

- *First, you have to sell it to a publisher through an editor.* The editors might even become very excited about your book. When this happens, they will then have to sell it to the marketing department (publishing is the only industry on the planet where the marketing department has so much sway over the products. In other industries, marketers are given products and told to use all of their considerable marketing skills to find a way to create a

market, but not so in publishing—don't get me started yet! (We'll discuss this further in the chapters on book marketing and promotion.) I would have to persuade this editor, to whom I had spoken on the phone, that she should take the next step with me.
- *Second, once the book is published, you have to sell the book to the book retailers.* Make no mistake; both you and your publisher will eventually have a role to play here. Of course, this was much more of an issue before the days of digital publishing. Getting your book into an online retail site is a piece of cake. However, it will just sit there among the millions of others. You will find it much more difficult if you want to see it in a bricks-and-mortar store.
- *Finally, when the book distribution channels (including booksellers) have it in hand—virtually and literally—you have to sell the book to your potential readers.*

But we will concentrate initially on the first time you have to sell a book because that's what your proposal is for: to sell it to a publisher.

I had an idea that I'd use my experience in the transplant and organ procurement business to write a book that would ask many questions. It wouldn't necessarily go so far as to answer them, since many of them were, up until then, unasked, and many had no real answers. I wanted to prompt people to think about the way organ transplantation was approached at the time. So, I had to ask myself a few critical questions.

- What was the real purpose of this book? What did I want to accomplish?
- How would I approach the topic? Did I have a theme?

- How would I organize the book? Would it have sections? Chapters? Stories?
- What kind of voice and style would I use? Would I use first person? Third? What reading level would I use?
- Why was I the best person to write this book? Would I have any credibility?
- What other books would be competitors?
- Who would actually read this book when it got to the bookstores?
- How could this kind of book be promoted to readers?

If I could answer those questions, I could write a detailed proposal whose purpose would be to persuade the editor (the acquisitions editor, to be precise) that this was a terrific book that I could write well and that readers would buy.

Here's what my proposal looked like:

The Patricia J. Parsons Approach to the Book Proposal

- A working title
- The book's theme and purpose
- What is this book about?
- The author
- Who are you, and why should the editor or readers trust you?
- The market
- Who will read this book?
- The competition
- What books are your competitors, and what makes yours unique?

- The promotion
- What will you do to promote it?
- The style & approach
- How will you organize this book, and what voice will you use?
- Sample chapters

WHAT IS THIS BOOK ABOUT? One of the most important aspects of writing—or perhaps selling—any book is being able to succinctly relate to anyone who asks exactly what the book is about. Some people call it the *elevator pitch*, but it's a bit more in-depth in a book proposal. In this section of the proposal, I include both theme and purpose. Although it might seem that the issue of theme is more appropriately associated with fiction than nonfiction, in my view, it is equally important in both genres. It's essential to consider how I want the reader to feel at the end of the book and what aspects of the emotional journey will lead them there. This is where the theme emerges. Although not so much the case with fiction, every nonfiction book needs to have a clear purpose. In other words, what is it designed to accomplish? What do I want readers to have experienced differently when they have finished the last page of the book?

THE AUTHOR: If I'm writing a nonfiction book, it only stands to reason that any editor, and subsequently any reader, will want to know what it is about me that makes me a credible source for this particular topic. When it comes to fiction, editors want to see if you can write, so telling them about your previous publications is useful. In addition, these days, for better or worse, publishers are often interested in your *platform*. This expectation is a tough one because it is true that even if you have thousands of friends on

Facebook and followers on Instagram and X, or even TikTok, there is no guarantee that even a fraction of these people will ever pay attention to you. This is the nature of the fractured attention span of the social media user. That being said, it can't hurt to consider this when describing yourself as the author of a particular book.

THE MARKET: Who am I writing this book for? Identifying your target readers is critically important in nonfiction because it helps determine the potential number of interested readers and where they can be found. However, it is also vital in terms of the actual writing. Knowing your potential audience helps you to focus your writing style. I'm not suggesting that you write *to* readers, but there are times when it's essential to have a grasp of their literacy level. An awareness of this information is especially vital when writing books aimed at young adults or children.

THE COMPETITION: This is an essential section for a publisher, but it also provides you, as the author, with a snapshot of what's already out there on this topic. I start with the big one—Amazon, for example—to research the kinds of material already on sale on related topics. Then, I begin to analyze the offerings to determine what's different about my approach. This is important for self-publishers. Later on, after you have finished writing and editing, and you begin the publishing process, you will want to become familiar with the categories in which your readers are most likely to discover your book. This early research can assist.

PROMOTION: I've said this before, and I will say it again throughout this book: what new authors fail to understand is that books do not sell themselves. They never have. They never will. Even at this early stage, it's important to consider what you will do or what a publisher could do with your help to promote this book. Will you speak at conferences where you could promote it? Do you have media connections? Could you write op-ed pieces at the time when you launch your book? Can you use your social media presence to promote it? It doesn't matter whether you publish through traditional publishers or do it all yourself. You will still have to be involved in promoting your book. You might as well address that in the beginning.

STYLE & APPROACH: This section outlines the voice I will use and creates a tentative table of contents. Once I have that well-organized list of contents, I will write a two- or three-paragraph description of every chapter.

When I wrote my first proposal, I had no idea whether all of the work to this point would pay off or not. It was finally ready to go to the publisher. Would she buy it based on the proposal? Would she ask to see the completed manuscript on spec? I had no idea. I knew I'd have to put in a lot of work before I had an answer. I learned how to write book proposals that publishers want.

At this point in my writing career, I'm now confident that I'd need one in any case, whether to meet a publisher's requirements or my own indie publishing ventures. In summary, exploring all of the questions posed above will help you shape your ideas into a book that might find an audience.

Self-Publishing and the book proposal question

So, you say you plan to self-publish. You think you don't need a book proposal to meet some agent or publisher's arbitrary requirements. I respectfully disagree. You need a proposal for yourself.

If you look closely at the proposal's outline, you'll see that producing it does several things.

- Book proposals require you to think carefully about the content of your book. This thinking allows you to determine if you have enough of a premise to build a complete book or just a magazine article or blog piece.
- Book proposals force you to examine your own credentials for producing this book. If you don't have a credible background, how will you convince readers to trust you?
- Book proposals demand that you be able to describe your book succinctly. You will need this information eventually when you develop promotional materials.
- Book proposals demand that you scrutinize your competition and target market. Again, you could go ahead and write without this. Still, if you plan to sell this book in the future (most writers are planning on selling if at all possible), you will be able to begin working on channels to get to these audiences even as you proceed through the writing process. Writers often long for diversions when writing (it's called procrastination), and what better distraction could there be than something that will enhance the future of the work you're putting off? Searching for marketing channels even before you finish writing and editing your book is a diversion from your writing when you need one, yet it will also pay dividends in the end.
- Book proposals demand that you outline your work and flesh out that outline. If you have never written a book from an outline before (and even if you have), you need to know that it's like having a GPS or a map to follow. It doesn't mean that you can't go off-course if you choose to do so, but it means that you have a sense of where you're going.

- Book proposals do not demand that you stick to them completely. It is the process of planning that will provide you with a foundation. Your book will inevitably take different turns, but this plan is something to come back to, thus avoiding the dreaded writer's block.

Fiction and the book proposal question

Although it is true that publishers or agents don't always ask for proposals for fiction, again, you're mistaken if you think you don't need one for yourself. I have recently noticed that fiction agents and publishers often use the term 'proposal' when describing submission requirements. You could just sit down to write (opening a vein, as many famous authors have suggested), but the blood will flow in a more workable fashion if it has a map. Yes, I know some writers are what the industry calls "pantsers," those writers who primarily write by the seat of their pants. However, this approach can produce interminable tears if you're a new writer.

Creating a map is like a little crutch that will prop you up. Probably, the map you create upfront will change dramatically as you move toward completing your project. Ideas do seem to flow as you write. You need to remember that a proposal is always a work in progress, regardless of genre or publishing model. It needs to be further shaped and massaged along the way. You will inevitably come up with new approaches, add content, remove content, and change chapters. However, with a written proposal/outline for yourself, you will be able to plunge into the process, knowing that you can extricate yourself and get back on track if you get stuck.

Lessons from writing my first book

The most important thing I learned from writing that first complete book was that I could do it. Then, I thought, if I could do it once, I could do it again. And again.

If you can complete a manuscript and do the work it takes to get it published, you will have a singular accomplishment in your life, regardless of the route to publication. If your book informs, educates or entertains others, you've left a legacy.

Let's create your legacy together.

Just remember what Sir James M. Barrie said about having his first book published: *"For several days after my first book was published, I carried it about in my pocket, and took surreptitious peeps at it to make sure the ink had not faded."* Remember J. M. Barrie? He was just the author of *Peter Pan*. You, too, can enjoy that thrill.

THREE

Becoming a Writer

"I'm a writer. I write not only for a living. I write because I'm a writer." ~ Gary Jennings

NOT EVERYONE WANTS TO BE A WRITER—sometimes, it just seems that way. Perhaps it's that so many people these days seem *to want to have written a book*—they seem to think it's easy. But what does it mean to be a writer? Are you a writer because you write? Or do you write because you're a writer? The answer to that question is crucial if you are actually a writer because it helps you move through the process, which is not, as your friends might think, easy. And if it's too easy, you're probably not doing it right. Let's talk about how we become writers.

A writer's beginnings

I had an odd experience a few years ago. I found myself peering into the mind of a fifteen-year-old girl, or perhaps it would be more accurate to say a fifteen-year-old writer. And the most peculiar thing of all is that it was me. Let me begin my story by taking you back to those days I spent in that children's library.

I was fifteen years old, a high school drama club aficionado and science nerd, yet I wanted nothing more than to be a novelist. Despite all my artistic yearnings, I also had a practical side, which won out in the university program selection process. In my senior year, I had my very best marks in biology, chemistry, and analytical trigonometry, so you can guess what I studied at university. And to tell you the truth, that health science degree and the Master of Science that followed have stood me in good stead throughout my career evolution from health communication, to health & business writer, to creative nonfiction writer, and now into fiction. But in high school, my English marks weren't far behind my math and science marks.

Every year, the students in grades eleven and twelve (juniors and seniors in the Canadian and American systems) were allowed to select a subject area to complete what was referred to as a "distinction project" in that subject. These days, some high schools refer to these projects as "theses," which is probably stretching the term a bit. After all, we are talking about high school. Nevertheless, it was an extra project whose successful completion would mean that I would have my "distinction" area noted on my final transcript. So, I decided to go for it.

I have no idea what my parents expected me to do, or even if they were completely aware that I was pursuing this path, but despite my strengths in math and science, I chose English. When I reflect on this now from the vantage point of my more senior years, it occurs to me that I didn't enjoy the way English was taught in high school at the time. In my view, there was far too much parsing of literature I would never have chosen to read (adult apologies to Hemingway, but *The Old Man and the Sea*?). Additionally, I had an English teacher whose interpretations of literary works were rarely in line with my own. And, as everyone knows, fifteen and sixteen-year-olds know everything. To be more specific about the focus of my project study, I chose the short story.

I had all but forgotten about the project until one morning a few years ago, when I took three magazine boxes off the highest shelf in my office to begin the laborious process of digitizing all my publications. The time had come to rid myself of the glut of paper that threatens to overtake most of us writers from time to time. What do you suppose was the first document that I pulled out? Much to my surprise, it was my grade eleven "distinction project."

The project's framework centred on aspects of the short story, a form that holds little interest for me as either a reader or a writer at this stage in my life. It's just a personal preference—I have nothing against short stories in general. The project, painstakingly typed on an actual typewriter (with only one or two whited-out typos), analyzed the short story's components. I wrote a short story that showcased each of the standard components' elements, including character, setting, plot, etc. The first story was character-driven; the next one relied heavily on the setting. The third was plot-driven. And on it went. But it was not this unusual approach to writing stories that fascinated me when I rediscovered my younger self in those pages. The overarching theme of each of the stories created the narrative of that fifteen-year-old writer. The theme that came through repeatedly, regardless of the actual characters or plot of the story, was this: *Know who you are and be true to yourself.*

When I think back through my day-job career and my writing by moonlight, I think that I have genuinely tried to do this myself—but I didn't realize that it was so deeply embedded in my psyche. The truth is that it has permeated much of my adult writing as well. It was kind of a light-bulb moment for me. After that trek down memory lane, I decided to continue it and re-read what I have long considered my very favourite novel of all time: *Rebecca* by Daphne DuMaurier.

American author Clifton Fadiman once said, *"When you re-read a classic, you do not see more in the book than you did before; you see more in you than was there before."* I do not doubt this.

I first read *Rebecca* when I was in high school, right around the time that I wrote those short stories. I had seen the various iterations of the movie based on it in the interim. Still, it was eye-opening for me to read this book so many decades later, trying to see what it was that captivated me and to figure out if the book had, in fact, had any influence on my writing. There is little doubt that, in the re-reading, I found out more about myself.

This time around, I found myself impatient with the narrator. A twenty-something woman of the 1930s, the unnamed protagonist, while visiting Monte Carlo, meets and then marries a much older and much more worldly man who subsequently takes her back to England to be the mistress of his estate, Manderley. Haunted by the ghost of her new husband's first wife, the young woman concocts in her mind all manner of scenarios to explain the first wife's death, most of which have absolutely no basis in reality. Indeed, the truth is much more sinister. As I re-read the book, I kept willing her to get over it, move on, and ask the questions that begged to be asked to clear up the uncertainties. I don't remember being so impatient with her when I was younger. So, I do think I've evolved as a woman. But what about as a writer?

Written in 1938, *Rebecca* was not a historical novel, the genre I have found myself drawn to both as a reader and as a writer in the last few decades. However, I read it near the beginning of the 1970s, so as a young woman, it was indeed historical, and I always thought about it that way. Daphne du Maurier did not need to create the world of the 1930s; she lived in it. But for me, the detail was now of historical significance, and I believe that this influenced my choice of genres.

I enjoyed the book the second time around, and I hope that some of my own work will stand the test of time as this one has. If you are truly a writer and not just someone who *wants* to write, you, too, will wish that your work could stand the test of time. The thought of someone picking up that book decades later and deriving some entertainment or enlightenment out of it is indeed enticing.

The notion of being true to yourself is as much a part of being a writer as it is a general life motto, and it is equally valid that what you read in your early years (and what you read as an older adult) shapes you as a writer, and in my view, that shaping never stops. I believe it's a worthwhile exercise for all of us who want to be published, regardless of genre, to think about what books moved us as children and what our favourite school subjects were. Think about this: Can you recall the very first piece of serious writing you ever produced? Are any of the books you read as a child or adolescent still on your bookshelves? Maybe it's time to revisit a few.

The books that shape us

As you have probably figured out by now, in my view, what we read as children and young adults has an enormous impact on what we choose to write as adults. If it doesn't, perhaps we're not being true to ourselves. It would make sense that it would, since what we read and experience influences us in many other ways (our beliefs, attitudes, etc.). Apart from my favourite book, *Rebecca*, I have had many others through the years, as I'm sure you have.

Another of these influential books is Anya Seton's classic historical novel *Green Darkness*.

I remember the *feeling* of the book more clearly than the *content* of the story. I remember being swept up in it as the characters moved from the twentieth century to the sixteenth century and back. I guess it's a bit of a romance, but the historical detail and the characters paint the picture for me. As I read it more recently, with the benefit of maturity (I guess), I'm struck by the writing this time around. Seton is a classic historical novelist who died in 1990, but not before writing more than a dozen books, many of which became bestsellers, and several were subsequently adapted into movies. But, back to my original musing: Has this book that I first read thirty years ago influenced my writing?

It probably has, but it's difficult to say which came first—the reading or the influence. Why did I choose the book in the first place? I think my sister recommended it, but if I were not interested in historical fiction, I would likely have ignored her—God knows I have ignored other recommendations she has made over the years!

So, there must have been something that compelled me to read and enjoy historical fiction at that time—long before I ever considered writing it. Somehow, though, that love of reading historical fiction has manifested itself in my love of research and writing in this area. This outcome is not the result of having studied history at university. As I mentioned earlier, I did not. So, if Anya Seton's work (after *Green Darkness*, I read several others, all of which I enjoyed) influenced me, what other kinds of books influenced me? Or at least, what are the most memorable books I read over the years?

I vividly remember a book called *Eighth Moon* by Sansan as told to Betty Bao Lord, which I notice now has a sub-title (I'm sure it did not have one when I read it—I wonder if we need sub-titles these days to select books?). The modern subtitle is *The True Story of a Young Girl's Life in Communist China,* and it takes me back a very long time. I know that I read many books back then, but this is the only one I remember vividly. I can recall particular aspects of the book, such as when Sansan, the memoir's author, had to work in fields where human feces were used as fertilizer. I could almost smell the atmosphere. That's going back a very long time in my life, since I read it in junior high school. I can only imagine how I found the story so divergent from my own life experience, given that the young woman in the story was about my age at the time. I can't articulate what it is about the book that makes it the only one I remember well from that point in my life, but I'm sure that remembering is reason enough to think it has influenced me somehow.

There is hardly a successful writer in the world, now or throughout history, who has not suggested that one must first and always be a reader to be a writer. What about you? What did you read as a child? As a young adult? What are you reading now?

As Stephen King once wrote, *"If you don't have time to read, you don't have the time (or the tools) to write. Simple as that."*

As you consider your own development as a writer through reading, consider the following questions:

- What is the first book you remember reading? How old were you?
- Why did you select that first book?
- What was your reaction to it?
- Did you continue to read in the same genre?
- If you moved on to other kinds of books, what were they? Why did you move on?

- What kind of stories are you compelled to tell as a writer?
- Were these influenced by what you read as a child? Young adult?
- What are you reading right now? (I will always assume that anyone who aspires to be a writer is always reading.)
- What would you like to be reading right now?
- What should you be reading right now?

Getting to know ourselves helps us to know which writing ideas that strike us from time to time have real depth for us and which are coming from outside influences that don't really reflect who we are. I submit that the ideas that come from who you really are will take you much further than those generated by external motivations, such as what you think might sell. Avoid this kind of approach to your writing at all costs. *Write what you love and what you're good at*, not what other writers in writing co-dependent groups (more about those later) suggest will sell.

"*You should write because you love the shape of stories and sentences and the creation of different words on a page. Writing comes from reading, and reading is the finest teacher of how to write.*" Or so said writer Annie Proulx.

Before we leave this self-examination, though, there is one more idea worth considering.

Maybe you shouldn't be a writer

Even if you don't want to go there, this is an idea that you should explore before publishing a book. If you're going to be a writer and are considering who you are as a writer, it might be a valuable exercise to reflect on all the reasons why you should *not write* a book. Or, perhaps more precisely, consider all the reasons you should *not publish* the book you write. If you do this and, at the end of the exercise, still believe that you should complete your book and work to get it published, you'll be stronger as you move through the process.

Lots of people have put together lists of why you shouldn't write. For example, Susannah Breslin, writing in *Forbes* online, suggests the following three reasons you shouldn't write: (1) you're not good at it; (2) it's too hard; and (3) it's too hard to make money. These are all valid points, in my view. What's so noteworthy is that in a later post, she says that her short piece on why you shouldn't be a writer is the one that readers hated most. It seems those who want to write a book don't want to be told the reasons why they shouldn't pursue it. But you do need to hear this before you move forward.

Blogger Karen Yates has a few more ideas about why you shouldn't write that book. She suggests that you back away from that computer if (1) you want to write because you think it will be fun or easy; (2) you want to write because you have a lot of Twitter followers; (3) you think the topic is one you think you can sell even if you're not passionate about it; (4) if you can't take criticism [I think you need to have a thick skin in general]; and/or (5) you're not willing to promote your book. Again, these are all valuable considerations.

After a couple of decades of writing books, I've determined that people should write if they want to: ***what they shouldn't necessarily do is publish***. If you're going to write, stop talking about it and write, remembering that it will be a difficult process, but go ahead regardless of what anyone tells you. Then take that manuscript and put it away to read in your dotage. Don't try to sell it to a publisher, and under no circumstances should you self-publish it. That is, unless you remember the following, which are my personal reasons that should give wannabe writers pause.

Do not publish your writing *if even one* of the following statements applies to you:

- You're writing as a form of catharsis. That's what your private, personal journals are for.
- You're writing because you're angry about something. At least don't publish anything until the anger subsides, and you can look at the matter more objectively.
- You're writing on a topic only because you think it will sell. If you are not passionate about it, it's not worth your time.
- You don't read. Any published writer worth his or her salt reads a lot and reads widely.
- You aren't willing to do the necessary research, regardless of genre.
- You aren't willing to work to continually improve your writing.
- You think that you'll simply sit down in front of the computer, and the words will flow.
- You can't stand revising and/or editing to the point that you don't do it.
- You don't have thick skin.
- You spend more time talking to others—in person and online—about your writing than you do writing.

Once you have looked inward and can honestly say that none of these statements apply to you, it's time to finish your book. But first, let's go back to where that book idea came from in the first place.

FOUR

In the Beginning was the Idea

"My ideas usually come not at my desk writing but in the midst of living." ~ Anais Nin

EMILY DICKINSON ONCE WROTE: *"The soul should always stand ajar, ready to welcome the ecstatic experience."* That, in a nutshell, speaks to every person who ever wanted to write a book or two or ten. We are always open to new experiences that lead to new thoughts and new writing ideas. I'm not a literary writer in the artistic sense of the word. I don't write literary novels or short stories. I write both fiction and nonfiction stories (and make no mistake, the nonfiction is based on storytelling in its finest sense) that result from an active process of seeking ideas. Once in a while, I stumble upon something, or I end up using an idea in a very different way than I started, but on balance, finding ideas is, for me, a very proactive process. So, accumulating ideas relies on knowing how to pay attention, which is the first step in the process. Step two requires a bit more discernment on our part as writers.

It's vitally important that we get it through our "writerly" heads that *not every idea is a good one.* Some ideas are meant to be contemplated, pondered over, perhaps written down in a journal and then tossed or at least put away—indefinitely. You will also find that you are not passionate about every idea you come up with, and if you are not excited about an idea, it is not worth your time. But just how *does* a writer find the idea that really ought to see the light of day?

My ideas come from a variety of places. In the past, some have come from a watercolour painting of a Titanic deck chair, a trans-Atlantic voyage on a Cunard Queen, an article in a medical journal (yes, indeed, one of my first novels was inspired by an article in a medical journal), or some other kind of academic journal.

A few years ago, I taught a course on creativity in corporate communication. During that course, we explored the notion of *paying attention,* which, in my view, is at the heart of finding that idea. Let's talk a bit about learning to pay attention to capture ideas and then develop your creativity further.

The beginning of the backstory

When precisely does a book's backstory begin? Does it start when the author says to herself, I should write a book about this? Does it begin when someone else says to a would-be author, you should write a book about that? In my experience, this latter situation happens more often with nonfiction. If an idea originates with someone else yet resonates with who you really are, and you can internalize it, the idea just might be a good one for you. Or perhaps the backstory of any given book begins even before that.

Is it when you come across an interesting kernel of an idea? A small article in a newspaper—the one you almost didn't read? Is it at the moment when that little piece of paper you clipped starts to invade your thoughts—unbidden? Is it when you are standing in the shower, pondering that throw-away comment an acquaintance made that you just can't shake? Is it when you, the would-be author, finally say not, 'I should write a book,' but, 'I want to write this book, and I'm going to write it'?

This issue of the germination of an idea was at the forefront of my mind when I pulled my car up in front of a watercolour artist's studio/home. A month earlier, I'd never even heard of this artist, but I had been haunted by one of the pieces featured in a brochure my husband had brought home after meeting her in his office.

The piece was a stark watercolour painting of a deck chair from the doomed ocean liner Titanic. The Titanic has a strong connection to the city where I was living at the time: Halifax, Nova Scotia, on Canada's Atlantic coast. Although the ocean liner went down closer to Newfoundland than to Nova Scotia, some of those who perished were brought to Halifax and buried in a cemetery in the city. Add to that the fact that there is a fascinating exhibit at the Maritime Museum of the Atlantic in Halifax focusing on the long-ago tragedy, and you have a storied port city that is deeply rooted in heartbreak.

However, there has always been something iconic about the single deck chair on display at the museum: it was indeed on the deck of the Titanic, and it was pulled from the icy waters of the North Atlantic. And beside this authentic deck chair, the one wounded by the tragedy and the ravages of time, sits a replica on which you can sit and contemplate what it must have been like out there in the dark waters of the icy North Atlantic. In any case, when I saw that thumbnail of the painting, I had to have it.

First, I had to find out if the artist still had the original. I didn't want a print; nothing less than the original would do. I contacted her, and although she couldn't put her hand on it at that exact moment, she assured me that she had not yet sold the original. When she asked me why I was interested, I spewed out an entire story about the deck chair, a painting that I'd seen on the wall of a bar on a cruise ship a couple of years earlier, and how I had an idea for a book set in about the 1920s or '30s on a transatlantic voyage (never mind that the Titanic went down in 1912). No doubt, she thought it was too much information! To be honest, I didn't have much of an idea yet, but it occurred to me that the idea was taking root. This is how it begins. I had the distinct feeling that this might just be the foundation of a backstory for a new book that I'd write in the coming years. I haven't written that book yet, but it may become one. As long as I continue to pay attention, the idea may have legs.

Paying Attention: Or how to attract ideas

The most accurate way to describe my mind is to use the Buddhist term *monkey mind*. That's me. My mind is constantly moving, the thoughts prattling on uncontrollably. Ideas fill my head from morning until night. This jumble can be problematic when I'm living other parts of my life, but it is usually how a writer's mind works. Here are some of the writing ideas that flashed through my brain in just one twenty-four-hour period.

I was doing some background fact-checking for the cover copy that one of my publishers had just sent along for my review of an upcoming book when I stumbled upon the biography of a woman named Christiane de Pisan. Never heard of her? Neither had I. She was a fourteenth-century writer, a woman ahead of her time, and a Venetian by birth. With my passion for historical fiction and a strong affinity for female characters, that sounded intriguing, which then got me wondering why I'd never heard of her before. In any case, I decided that there was a story there just waiting to be told. A new book, perhaps?

On the same day, while working on a document for my day job, I stumbled upon another interesting idea: maybe I should write something about how university students want to be entertained by their professors these days. Interesting.

Then, there are the inevitable ideas that always spring to mind when I'm getting ready to go on a vacation. Since we are avid travellers in our family, this is usually ongoing throughout any given year. A story set in London or New York? On Broadway, perhaps? Well, you get the idea.

Here's the thing, though. *To truly capture ideas, you need more than a sturdy journal or two. You need to quiet your mind and pay attention.* For me, the only way to do that was to take a meditation class, which I did some years ago. I don't meditate every day—although I really should—but the techniques I learned help quiet that monkey mind a bit. Only when my mind is a bit more peaceful can I truly capture any single idea that flies across my brain. I just have to sit still for a while. It might work for you.

According to experts on such matters, a wandering mind is a characteristic that makes us human. However, it is also what makes it so difficult for many (perhaps most?) of us to pay attention for any length of time. And these days, we have even more temptations that carve up any attention we do have. If you spend time on social media, talking on the phone, texting and reading texts, you don't have time to be in your own head. And sometimes, that's exactly where a writer needs to be. It's probably where a writer needs to be a lot of the time. Consider all of those people walking down a city street with their heads tilted downward into that tiny screen. Are they paying attention to their surroundings? Their thoughts? They are not.

A few years ago, I decided to learn to focus my attention on details. Small details. It had occurred to me that these little details would enrich my writing. I knew that this skill could be learned, but I had to find something that required this kind of detail orientation. I decided to take a drawing class.

I do not have a shred of talent for that kind of visual expression. I seem to have some flair for graphic art and have done a fair bit of that over the years, but picking up a drawing pencil was very foreign to me. I was determined, though, so I persevered with the classes.

The class began with a drawing exercise, of course. This very first exercise required us to draw a half-peeled banana. Have you ever really looked at a half-peeled banana? I mean, really looked at it? The banana sits there on the table, half-naked. The banana peel has separated into three strips. One falls on the table, one flops on the banana, and the third is behind and has that little black part of the stem on it. And the light and shadows are even more interesting. The banana has so much variation. And I had to sketch it. To do that, though, I had to examine the banana and its skin in minute detail.

Later, I had to draw an avocado. Take a close look at an avocado sometime. It's a series of intricate light and shadow, and reproducing a picture of it requires keen observation.

The most important lesson I learned was that to be a visual artist, you have to be *very* observant. You're looking at infinite variations in light and shadow, but you can't see that unless you look closely. Even if your artwork resembles Picasso's later works with all of those deconstructed images, you still need to be keenly observant. Until I visited the Picasso Museum in Barcelona some years ago, I had no idea that Picasso had not always been an abstract painter. His early work was very realistic. All of his work required a considerable focus on details, regardless of the artistic product at the end.

I did learn to pay attention to visual details, and I did learn to draw. I've often used this new skill in paying attention to the details of the people around me. These are the minutiae that often later make their way onto a page, to buildings that need to become part of my settings, to clouds that need to help me set a mood. It still seems funny that I improved my narrative description by learning to draw. The bottom line is that I now (sometimes) pay closer attention.

We live in a soup of ideas. We are surrounded and enveloped by them. We just have to pay attention.

When inspiration strikes

As I mentioned, our family travels often and far. In the past five years, we've been to Tahiti and the South Pacific islands, Australia, Peru, Ecuador, Chile, Hong Kong, China, Japan, Italy, Greece, Turkey, Malta, and, of course, lots of Caribbean islands (I'm a Canadian. The winters are long). And we never miss an opportunity to travel to the U.S. In the five years before that, we travelled to the U.K. (three times), France (four times), Monaco (at least five times—my son worked there), and lots of other parts of Europe. We love to be inspired by geography and cultures that are foreign to us. I believe that newness, freshness, and novelty are the fundamental characteristics of inspirational activities. It may be something completely unfamiliar or simply a new perspective on something familiar. Either way, a writer needs to be looking for something new. Vacations, for me, have "inspiration" value. My settled mind has permitted new ideas to bubble to the top of my consciousness when I return. However, not everyone travels, so every writer's opportunity to experience newness is different. You have to actively seek out what *inspires* you.

In medical terms, *inspiration* means breathing in and breathing out. In a way, artistic inspiration is the same. The writer (or choreographer, painter or even corporate strategist, for that matter) has a sudden burst of creativity—the genesis of that moment might not even be discernible at the time. The creator only knows that something has triggered action. So, in a way, it's like breathing in and breathing out—the creative fodder is breathed in, and the creative output is breathed out. Over the years, however, various creative individuals have had differing takes on just what it means to be inspired. There are lessons for writers in those differing perspectives.

LESSON 1: American composer, conductor and author Leonard Bernstein once said, *"Inspiration is wonderful when it happens, but the writer must develop an approach for the rest of the time...The wait is simply too long."* Don't just sit back and wait for the muse to strike. Find ways to actively seek inspiration in the meantime. You can use meditation, walking, running, reading, painting, or even web surfing through places you enjoy (not social media sites!).

LESSON 2: Many artists echo painter Pablo Picasso's approach to the creative process. He said, *"Inspiration exists, but it has to find us working."* Just get down to work. Write about anything around you, and eventually, the creative muse will strike. You'll be inspired to trash everything or use it in new and innovative ways.

LESSON 3: American businessman Nolan Bushnell has said, *"The ultimate inspiration is the deadline."* Mundane, perhaps, but so crucial to a writer. Set deadlines and stick to them. Try this: tell your significant other or someone whose feedback on your writing you appreciate that you'll have a few chapters to be read in two weeks. Even that kind of deadline is inspirational. Then, when you have a deadline from a publisher, you'll know how to seek inspiration from knowing it has to get done. (We'll return to this discussion of the beauty of deadlines in Chapter Nine.)

Artist and writer Julia Cameron wrote: *"In order to have a real relationship with our creativity, we must take the time and care to cultivate it."*

Turn off your autopilot

Most of us walk around on automatic pilot most of the time. Research suggests that up to 80% of our lives is spent functioning in this state—not truly paying attention to where we are and what we are doing. Being *intentional* in your activities is a key part of learning to use your creativity.

Lots of people have written about what it takes to be creative. Here's my list of the ***Eight Habits of Highly Creative People***.

1. *You need to believe that you are creative and that creativity is not the sole purview of the so-called creative geniuses*. Perhaps now would be a good time to start believing that there is no such thing as a creative genius.
2. *You need to be prepared to create*. Every day, you need to be ready to create.

3. *Pay attention to what is going on around you.* This follows immediately from being prepared, so you need to do it every day for the rest of your life!
4. *Broaden your interests.* Learn something new. Read something different. Write something different than your usual, even if it's just a short piece. Keep a special journal for this activity.
5. *Make the time and space in your life to be creative.* Time is an issue that will continue to haunt you. How will you find the time in your busy life to be creative? You just will. You must.
6. *Remember what it was like to be a kid.* Kids are the most imaginative members of our species. So, you have to forget how much you know—how much you've learned and experienced since you were a child—because these things will be too sensible.
7. *Be tenacious.* Don't give up. Stick to the challenge until you get it.
8. *Be willing to take risks.* Stick your neck out. Stop caring what other people think of you. The truth is that anxiety about what others will think of your ideas is one of the most common obstacles to creativity.

Descartes once said, *"It is not good enough to have a good mind; the main thing is to use it well."* Being inspired by a new idea is a rush for any writer. Remember, though. N**ot all ideas are good ones**—you don't pursue everything.

FIVE

You Are What You Write

"Every secret of a writer's soul, every experience of his life, every quality of his mind, is written large in his works." ~ Virginia Woolf

WHAT YOU WRITE SAYS A LOT ABOUT YOU as a person and writer in the twenty-first century. There was a time when writers wrote about their passions, whether historical fiction, crime stories, biographies, or travel, to name but a few. I'm going to suggest that writing about your passions is still what will make you a successful (or at least happy) writer, but books these days are increasingly written with the primary purpose of making money.

Over and over, online writing gurus—especially those who criticize the traditional publishing model—suggest that you just have to figure out what readers want and write that, regardless of what you truly want to write. Once again, I have to say it: if this is your main reason for wanting to write those books, you will not achieve real success. You are not really a *writer*; instead, you are a *content creator*. These are not the same things. There is nothing wrong with being a content creator, but you must own it. Then, if you really want to be a writer, write what inspires you. Although

I believe you may learn a great deal from this book if you are a content creator, don't kid yourself (or others) by suggesting that you're a writer or author in the truest sense. You might sell books, but you will never be fulfilled as a writer. There is a great deal of wisdom to the old notion that if you do what you love, the money will follow.

What I write: Writing across genres

It may come as a surprise to students I've had over the years—those who sat in my classes to learn about communication ethics or strategy. However, I began my unexpected academic career as a writing teacher. I never intended to be a university professor. I was an accidental academic.

I had always been interested in teaching and thought it was probably one of my strengths. I had done it for several years in a previous incarnation. I had taught anatomy and physiology, ethics, and human sexuality to nursing students before my career evolved into health and medical communication, eventually leading to writing books and teaching communication (specifically public relations and corporate communication). However, by that time, with one published book and numerous feature pieces under my belt, I initially went to the university as a writer who could teach writing part-time.

The first course I taught—before I ever even considered teaching full-time—was called "Print Media: Planning and Writing." It focused on bedrock corporate writing in those days: newsletters, annual reports, brochures, op-eds, and other promotional pieces. There is no such course with that title these days. However, its descendant, "Text-Based Media," comes close and now includes special considerations in writing for the web in general and social media in particular. It's something different to write a 3000-word feature article than it is to craft a 140-character tweet (or whatever we're calling it these days on X). However, doing either of these well involves understanding how we communicate through the written word. Over the next few years, I also taught news and feature writing and persuasive writing after the department's then-chairman talked me into applying for a full-time job. But I never intended to stay.

My temporary foray into academia lasted twenty-six years. So, what's the lesson here?

For me, it means that our skill sets can cross many disciplines. In writing, this means that these skills can cross different genres. However, the term 'writing across genres' has two distinct meanings. First, let's talk about individual writers writing across genres. Then, we'll talk about those genres that cross over into other genres.

German writer Goethe is said to have opined that *"every author in some way portrays himself [sic] in his works, even if it be against his [sic] will."* This observation either defines a symptom of mental confusion or perhaps the hallmark of an interesting personality for someone who writes in various genres. I'd like to think that, in my case, it's the latter.

The truth is that I started my writing career as a medical writer. Skills honed in that specialty led me into medical communication more broadly (I also earned a graduate degree in this area), which eventually morphed into general communication: most of my past work has been writing about health and corporate communication. But I'm a *writer*, first and foremost. That means that I can use my skills to write anything that resonates with me. I decided to try my hand at narrative nonfiction, which led to my first book sale to a publisher, as I mentioned earlier. When I felt I had a more personal story to tell, I wrote a memoir. I then took my research skills into an area that I love to read—historical fiction.

In my view, like everyone else, writers have particular strengths, and my strengths are not the same as yours. I think it's crucial for you to know your strengths and figure out how to use them across genres. For example, my meticulous research skills, honed while writing nonfiction (not to mention academic research), have been enormously helpful in moving into historical fiction. Story-telling is also a strength that many of us have—it's a skill that is important both to nonfiction (creative or otherwise—narrative or prescriptive, as the book trade calls it) and fiction writers.

The second way you can think about the concept of "writing across genres" is that discrete categories of writing can be "mashed up" to use the current jargon to create a cross-genre genre. Make sense?

Here's my example: I have a secret—I sometimes read chick-lit, and I'm not apologizing for it. I sometimes like a bit of escapist reading from time to time, but only if it's well-written, like some chick-lit is. I am also interested in creating some of my own and have done so. However, I have noticed a bit of a formula to much so-called chick-lit, and that's not the kind of writing that interests me. I'm interested in reading and writing chick-lit that doesn't necessarily follow the genre's conventions. In the end, perhaps it's not chick-lit at all because of that. So, I combined my interest in travel and travel writing with my interest in chick-lit to write a travel-focused chick-lit book. Is this a cross-genre? Maybe, but who's to say? Who is the arbiter of what is and is not a genre? And who says that because my book is funny, with a young, modern woman as the protagonist, it's chick-lit anyway? Maybe it's just women's literature, a term that sounds a bit more grown-up but perhaps fails to capture the imagination! That's why I call it "lit-for-intelligent-chicks."

In any case, cheers to coming up with your own genres and writing whatever moves you.

"Write what you know": An outdated concept?

The origin of the admonishment to a writer to "write what you know" has been variously attributed to Mark Twain and Ernest Hemingway, among others. I suppose they would have come by the idea honestly and can thus be forgiven for it. After all, both of them primarily wrote about places and things with which they were intimately involved. It would have seemed like a good thing to both of them. But is this a good way for a writer to proceed along the writing journey? Is it necessary? I don't think so, in either case.

A few years ago, I was quite taken by B.S. Shapiro's extraordinary novel, *The Art Forger*. Not to give it away (because you really ought to read it), it's the story of an aspiring artist who makes her living wage doing reproductions of famous artworks that are sold as that: copies. She does copies, not forgeries—which is all about the intent of the piece.

I picked the book up in the first place because it is at least partly about Edgar Degas' work. I've been 20,000 words into a manuscript that revolves around Degas' ballerina sculptures for some years now. I put it on the back burner while I finished other writing pieces for publication (and, in the meantime, noting that I'm not the only writer of historical fiction who has found this an interesting subject). To say that I'm a devotee of Degas' work might be stretching it a bit, but I am a fan, and I find some of the unanswered questions about historical characters too tantalizing to ignore.

As I read Shapiro's book, I felt myself becoming very educated about the fine points of both the art and the science of oil painting. I relied on the author of this fictional piece to have done her homework: I wanted to believe in the details that made the story feel authentic and vibrant. But I always kept in the back of my mind that this is a work of fiction. So, the question remains: where is the line between fiction and fact drawn in these kinds of tales, and does it matter?

Most authors whose fictional work touches on real people, places and things take great pride in doing their homework. As a result, there is usually a note in the book, as mentioned above, indicating the line where researched facts give way to the writer's imagination. So, what, you might reasonably ask, does this have to do with the question of whether or not we should take heed of the old adage, "Write what you know"? It occurs to me that in these days of the World Wide Web, we can "know" a great deal more than we used to, or at least we can think we do.

There was a time when doing research was much more difficult and time-consuming. If you're as old as I am, you might remember slogging to the library to comb through real reference guides, real books, and real documents page after page. If you remember researching on microfiche, you're probably as old as I am. I have to say that I think back on those days with fondness. I truly enjoyed those hours spent among the great tomes crammed with information just aching to get out. The trouble was just how long it took to find that information that would provide those all-important nuggets to add depth and breadth to a piece of writing. Finding information is almost instantaneous these days, but knowing if it is credible is a bit more challenging.

The truth is that today, we can become semi-experts in many topics if we know how to conduct research and are willing to spend the time.

Writing in the *New York Times*, Ben Yagoda, author of *How to Not Write Bad: The Most Common Writing Errors and the Best Ways to Avoid Them* and a faculty member in the English Department at the University of Delaware, clarifies for us as follows:

> *"Writers who are intimately familiar with their subject produce more knowing, more confident and, as a result, stronger results...the idea is to investigate the subject till you can write about it with complete confidence and authority. Being a serial expert is actually one of the cool things about the very enterprise of writing..."*

And therein lies the wonder of these days of information overload. For writers, this overload is among the essential tools in our toolboxes. As with all tools, the trick is to become an expert at using them.

As my own writing segued from nonfiction into fiction, I've been forever grateful for the research skills I could hone through the years. For any of us who are writing fiction with a basis in fact, those skills are crucial to the authentic voice we all seek. The bottom line is that we all think we "know" many things these days. My question to you is this: Do you really know how you came to "know" what you think you "know"? Stay with me here.

How we know things

There is a fancy word for the science of "knowing." That word is *epistemology*. People who study epistemology try to figure out how we, as humans, come by our knowledge. How could this possibly be important to a writer? Although these philosophers are more interested in what *knowledge* is, how we acquire it is important to us as writers. Having the actual, personal experience of something is only one of those ways, which is generally how the admonition to "write what you know" is usually interpreted. I'm suggesting that it isn't the only way.

The four traditional "ways of knowing" are as follows:

- *Intuition:* Using your intuition means using rationalization to come to "know" something. If someone were to ask you how you know what you think you know in this way, you would answer, "Because it stands to reason." Have you ever said that? It is true that sometimes, we just figure things out. If this is how you know something, it would be open to criticism since someone else's reasoning might lead to a different conclusion. However, if you're writing a detective novel, it might be helpful.

- *Tenacity:* When someone tenaciously hangs on to ideas, telling you that he or she "knows" something to be true even in the face of overwhelming evidence to the contrary (there is much of this going on in the public these days, don't you think?), this person is said to know by tenacity. Just because someone says he or she knows something doesn't necessarily make it a fact. In this kind of knowing, if asked how you know what you know, you might answer, "Everyone knows that." Common knowledge? Maybe, but it could just as easily be simply "the way it's always been." Again, it may not truly be a fact, and others might just as easily say to you, "No, not everyone knows that." But it is a kind of knowledge that we rely on perhaps more often than we should.

- ***Authority:*** Knowing by authority means that your "knowledge" is based on your interpretation of the source's credibility. You find an expert to interview; you use a credible internet source; you find a book written by an expert in the field. These are extremely useful ways for authors to develop knowledge about their subject matter. In fact, it's often crucially important. Remember, though, even when dealing with so-called experts or authoritative sources, you might find others who dispute the "facts." Indeed, this very notion is the basis for one of my historical novels: an academic authority on ancient music challenged the long-held belief that the eleventh-century Catholic mystic Hildegard of Bingen composed some seventy-plus pieces of music attributed to her. That led me to ask: what if someone else had really composed them? Of course, I had to come up with an answer, which is where history segues into historical fiction.

- ***Science:*** The scientific approach to knowing things is based on empiricism—sensory experience—and a method of gathering that data that is highly formalized in an effort to rule out competing explanations. At least, that's how scientists use the theory of empirical data gathering. As writers, we base our empirical research on our personal experiences. As long as we don't use these experiences to draw conclusions about others in the same situation, the knowledge we gain from them is valid for us and becomes the basis for much literature.

Your empirical information is, in fact, "what you know," and it will serve you well, and, as I mentioned earlier, it is often what people mean when they tell you to "write what you know." Just remember that it isn't the only way to *know* things! So, the bottom line is that the notion, in its literal sense, that you must write only about what you "know" is, in fact, an old cliché. However, a writer does need a deep level of knowledge about the subject matter and sometimes, that involves facts.

For example, I used Costa Rica as a setting for a part of a novel I wrote a few years ago. Yes, I had travelled to the Central American country (remember how inspired I am by travel?). Even though I had been there, I still had to do a lot of background research on coffee growing before I could incorporate it into my book. I had to know a lot more about the background than I would ever need to use in the pages of the book. So, you do have to know what you're writing about. You just don't have to write only about what you know before starting.

Bret Johnston, a writer who also teaches writing, suggests that he uses his own experiences as a kind of "scaffolding" for his work. If this were not the case, no woman could ever write from a man's point of view or vice versa. No one could set a story in a time or place the author had never visited. As a result, much literature, including historical fiction, for example, would never exist.

Science fiction writer Robert J. Sawyer once said, "*The heart and soul of good writing is research; you should write not what you know but what you can find out about.*"

Are you a "real" writer?

I was having lunch at a favourite local restaurant when I overheard a man at an adjacent table chatting about what he'd been up to lately. He mentioned the word *writing*, and, naturally, my attention was drawn to his subsequent remarks.

"I dream of being a writer," he said. "But not of writing."

And therein lies the crux of the problem facing writing and publishing today. Everyone wants to be a writer, but few are willing to do the hard work it takes to be one.

In some circles, you cannot be a "real" writer unless you have a Master's degree in Fine Arts. This argument suggests that you need that literary training to activate your writing talent fully, and only those with that massive writing talent are real writers. That's probably outdated as much as it is elitist. No, I don't think you need an MFA to be a real writer, although having been schooled in the elements of the language that are the tools of the trade is probably a job requirement.

In 2019, British journalist and critic Hermione Hoby wrote a piece in the *New Yorker* on the relevance of the MFA to real writing. In it, she contends that "… bad writers are everywhere, bred by MFA programs across the country, turning out banal, interchangeable stories." It appears that from Hoby's perspective, the professionalization of the writing craft by these kinds of programs doesn't seem to have done much to improve the overall writing available to readers. She also concludes that, rather than following the dictum "Write what you know," that we have already examined, as writers, we should invest in what she refers to as an "honest combination of curiosity and humility," which poses a better question: "What *can* I know?"

Just as you would for any other pursuit, you need to take any talent you have, nurture it by learning as much as possible about your craft, and then work hard. You may be searching for that magic bullet, that instant formula for success, but it doesn't exist. If you want to win a gold medal in downhill skiing, you don't search for a shortcut to success because you know it doesn't exist. Writing is no different.

So, if you need a book that will give you the three sure-fire steps to authorial success, you've come to the wrong place. The next section of this book is about work—all that hard work you'll have to do to be a writer.

Reality Check #2

Talent is not Enough: Writing is Hard Work

"There is nothing to writing. All you do is sit down at a typewriter and bleed."
~ Ernest Hemingway

"Writing is hard work and bad for the health." ~ E. B. White

SIX

Cross-Training for Writers: Getting Ready for the Marathon

"The role of the artist is to ask questions, not answer them."
~Anton Chekhov

I DOUBT THERE IS ANYONE AMONG US who hasn't come across a magazine, newspaper article, or online post about cross-training. After all, we're all obsessed with fitness these days, *n'est ce pas*? Not you? Even so, I'll bet that you still have a pretty good idea about what cross-training is. It's an approach to fitness that involves various training methods to improve your overall fitness. For example, if you usually run for its health benefits, you'll improve your overall fitness by adding strength training, which is likely to improve your running. You already know this. But have you ever thought that the same approach might apply to your writing?

It doesn't matter if most of your writing is on a blog, in magazines, in academic journals or even in your personal journal: **HOW YOU WRITE MATTERS**. How you write affects how you and others understand your ideas. As William Zinsser (whose book *On*

Writing Well should be in your library) suggested, "*Most people have no idea how badly they write.*"

Cross-writing to enhance your writing

Take a few moments to go back to read some of your very earliest writing. You'll quickly notice that if you've kept on with it, your writing today is likely much better than it was when you started. Your continual practice has, in fact, made you better. But if you've gone a step further by actively working at improving your writing, it will jump off the page at you and scream: "I am better!" One of the most under-appreciated approaches to writing improvement, in my view, is the concept of ***cross-writing***.

I'm not sure when I came up with or stumbled on the idea, but it probably had something to do with that creativity course I taught a few years ago to a small group of third-year university students. In that course, we explored the idea of ***creativity cross-training***: for example, if you're a choreographer, you could try a visual art like photography or painting to keep the creative juices flowing and to learn to see things in different ways. This enhances your creativity. The same holds for writing.

I have great respect for authors who work in a particular specialty, but I'll bet my next paycheque that most of them (if not all) do at least a bit of cross-writing even if they don't cross-publish (not sure that's a real concept for anyone but me). Many, if not most, authors keep journals in which they write a lot of material they never intend for readers to see. Or at least they used to. Sometimes, I get the impression that many of today's writers think that everything they write should be published and that it is all worthy of publication. I beg to differ.

In any case, many authors also cross-write alongside their journaling. But I'm talking about a more major commitment to this approach than simply journaling in a different genre.

I'm talking to all of you writers who don't seem to think that your writing needs to improve—that it's "good enough." It's not: *good enough is never good enough*. You need to continually work to improve your writing if you are a writer. If you are a dabbler, ignore this advice and continue to dabble. But for the sake of the readers out there, don't publish.

It's my view that if you are a nonfiction writer, taking the time to write a bit of fiction, blog, or even keep a personal journal would help. You would improve your storytelling ability. Despite the parameters within which you must publish your nonfiction, at the heart of what you're doing is telling the story of your research, your theory, or your opinion. In addition, the sheer act of writing continually improves its fundamental quality.

On the other hand, if you are primarily a fiction writer, try your hand at writing an op-ed piece or a how-to document. Write about a personal journey in your private journal or share it on your blog. Again, this is not necessarily for public consumption.

I'm also talking to all those bloggers who free-associate in every blog post. I'm imploring you to take the time to do some research, check your facts, and craft a more authoritative piece. I'm not necessarily suggesting that you post it on your blog – instead, do it for yourself and your writing.

Perhaps all of this is to justify my own approach to writing. Over the years, I've done a bit of academic writing, a lot of business writing, some blogging, a few nonfiction trade books, a couple of textbooks, a bit of creative nonfiction (memoir) and, increasingly, works of fiction. I like to think of this apparent lack of focus as evolutionary in terms of my own writing quality. I often go to my bookshelf and take down a copy of the first book I ever managed to entice a publisher to publish. I look at it, remembering how I felt when I first held it in my hands. I have to admit I was pretty proud. However, when I pluck up the courage to open the pages and read a bit of it, I am usually astounded that a publisher bought it. I believe my writing is much better now and continues to improve with every article, every blog post and every book I write. I don't think you can ever stop improving. Nor should you want to do so. [I'll talk more about writing practice in Chapter Eight.]

What can you learn from cross-writing?

I learned a lot from my forays into different genres. Specific skills honed in one genre became very useful when moving back to styles I'd dabbled in previously. I'd recommend at least a journal-worthy foray into other genres, even for writers who have a laser-like focus on one form of writing. It's unnecessary to publish in different genres; instead, it's important to use those sessions just as writing practice. What skills did I learn by writing in one genre that I could use to improve another style?

In the early years of my writing career, I wrote many feature articles—profiles, health stories, and lifestyle stories primarily for magazines. One of the first things you have to do to write a feature is to organize your material and write an outline. That ability to think about telling a story has improved my writing of case studies in textbooks, for example. Also, interviewing skills are essential for gathering first-hand information and for human interest (clearly, you can't write a profile piece without being able to do this!). Learning how to interview in person, over the phone, via Zoom or FaceTime or even via email is a meaningful way to gather information for writing in many, arguably all, genres. For example, if you are writing historical fiction, highly developed interviewing skills will allow you to glean more useful information from sources you approach for their expert knowledge. This also holds true in writing police procedurals, murder mysteries, and even stories set in different places and cultures. I can't think of a single writing focus where excellent interviewing skills wouldn't help you.

What's more is that doing interviews helps you with your writing when you have to take the material and shape it into something more than a Q&A transcript. No one likes those, you know, not even in magazines. But if you haven't had the benefit of education or experience in interviewing, how do you get better?

Here are a few suggestions.

- Before preparing your interview questions, expect to do some background research on your subject and your area of expertise.
- Have an objective in mind when you begin. What would you like to take from this interview/what is the one big question you want or need to have answered?
- Prepare your questions in advance. This is one time where "pantsing" will not bode well.
- Be prepared, however, to follow your subjects when they veer off course. Let them go to see where it takes you. Just know when to rein it in. Sometimes, the best material comes from those asides.
- Be prepared to pay attention and ask follow-up questions whenever your interview subject takes one of those side journeys.
- Learn to take good notes.
- Transcribe your notes and/or recordings immediately after the interview.

- Leave it for a day or two, then come back to figure out the "good stuff."
- Practice on friends and family.

Earlier, I mentioned that learning to tell a story helped me write textbook case studies. That ability to tell a story also became extraordinarily useful in writing the memoir. Feature articles that use anecdotes, which are nothing more than mini-stories, are more vivid than those without this device. And, of course, as I moved from nonfiction writing into fiction writing, all that focus on learning storytelling has to be seen as beneficial, don't you think?

The self-reflection skills I had to engage in to write the memoir became a key to opening my imagination to the rich possibilities of fiction in an academic journal article. Twice now, scholarly pieces have sparked my imagination for fictional stories, and I hope this happens again.

The research skills I honed by writing textbooks are the key to my ability to write historical fiction full of accurate historical detail. I can zip through library databases, ferreting out essential and exciting background that generally adds to both the backstory and the main story.

And, of course, all the editors who have had a crack at my work have taught me some of the fine points of grammar, punctuation and style—even if I had to argue with them from time to time. In almost all cases, they won.

All of this makes me a writer who I think continues to improve, but one who has not yet arrived.

It would be worth examining your current writing to see if you could improve by trying out another form.

SEVEN

Shaping Ideas: Reading, Writing and Keeping Journals

"The greatest part of a writer's time is spent in reading, in order to write; a man will turn over half a library to make one book."
~ Samuel Johnson

YOUR INSPIRATION AND IDEAS are only the beginning. They need shape. Although there are many ways that artists, innovators, and thinkers shape ideas, in my view, there are a few that are specific to the craft of writing. This chapter focuses on the two approaches that I believe are key to shaping writing ideas: reading and journaling.

Both reading and journaling are activities that keep a writer's well filled. You're not reading to steal other people's ideas (although it has often been said that there are no new ideas). Instead, you are reading to expose your mind to various points of view, genres, styles, and voices. All of this helps you to shape your ideas. Then, as you work in your journal, you have a chance to begin to put those ideas into various shapes to see what comes out—what is usable versus what is just practice. Writing teacher Natalie Goldberg, the author of *Writing Down the Bones* and other important books about her approach to the writer's craft, said this: *"Writing is the act of discovery."*

What should you read?

What does a writer read? And perhaps even more important, what *should* a writer read?

Both questions make the reasonable assumption (as we've discussed previously) that writers do read. Anyone serious about writing something worth reading would not argue with that. Indeed, if you don't read, I implore you not to write. At all. End of discussion.

Perhaps you think that writers should read about writing. Of course, as a writer, you can benefit from reading writing handbooks and style guides. These prescriptive materials offer a bit of self-help for writers.

Perhaps you think that writers should read books in their specialty area (for example, if you're a creative nonfiction writer, you should read creative nonfiction; if you're a historical novelist, you should read historical novels; if you're a women's lit writer, that's what you should read and so on). Of course, you need to read the kind of literature that you write. In fact, it's probably more important the other way around: you should probably write what you like to read (rather than what you think will sell, as some writing gurus suggest). So, it's likely that you will read all of this anyway. But in my view, it's only part of what you should read.

I think it's also essential to cross-read. This diverse reading is a natural extension of the concept of creativity cross-training, as we discussed in the last chapter. Reading in genres far afield from your everyday work and writing is one of the best ways to keep your creative mind working overtime. And it's relatively easy to tell if you're a cross-reader. Stack up the books you are currently reading and the books you have on your next-to-read list and see what's there.

Here's a snapshot of one of my "current-reading stacks" from a few years ago.

At that time, I was reading Steig Larsson's trilogy, which was popular then. I was on the final one, *The Girl Who Kicked the Hornet's Nest*, so that one was in the stack. Also in the pile was *London Day-by-Day*, which represents my favourite way to prepare for a trip. I had been to London several times before. Still, my husband and I were planning to meet our son, who was then living in Europe, there for a few days before ticking off one of the experiences on our bucket list that he would join us for: a transatlantic liner crossing from London to New York on the *Queen Mary 2*. That little travel book series is my bible for walking new areas of cities. Sometimes, they are even helpful when I'm writing about those cities. You'd be surprised how handy travel guides can be in doing research for settings—even ones you've visited.

No Exit and Three Other Plays by John-Paul Sartre is a bit outside my usual reading, but it was also in the stack. I had not read a play for a very long time. However, one of my hobbies is writing ballet librettos, and I promised my son, a nascent choreographer, a new one. All my life, I've been inspired by Sartre's notion that *"Hell is other people."*

Health Communication—what can I say? This textbook was also on the stack then because I was working on developing a new course in my department. You probably have to do some reading about your line of work from time to time. Don't discount that. It can also provide background for your future writing.

Finally, there was a book called *Purses,* which represents one of my passions: handbags. The truth is that one of the antique handbags I came across in my cross-reading is the inspiration for a future historical novel.

See, what did I tell you about cross-reading? What are *you* reading now?

Reading suggestions to get you started

If you do an online search for books that writers should read, you'll come up with various types of lists. There are lists of writing manuals that are helpful in honing the craft part of the process. There are lists of the best fiction that every fiction writer ought to read. These are useful for beginning to hear what great writing sounds like. There are lists of memoirs by writers about themselves and their lives. These are fascinating reads for writers. Learning about the creative process as nurtured by other writers, especially those you admire, can be very inspiring. I think you need to read all these kinds of books.

Here are some books that I think you could reasonably begin with.

- *On Writing Well* by William Zinsser. This book should be number one on your list.
- *Starting from Scratch: A Different Kind of Writers' Manual* by Rita Mae Brown
- *Writing Down the Bones* by Natalie Goldberg
- *Bird by Bird: Some Instructions on Writing & Life by* Anne Lamott
- *If You Want to Write* by Brenda Ueland
- *One Writer's Beginning* by Eudora Welty

Reference books you should have at your fingertips:

- *The Elements of Style* by Strunk & White
- *The Elements of Grammar* by Margaret Shertzer
- *The Elements of Editing* by Arthur Plotnik
- *The Sense of Style* by Steven Pinker (a modern update that addresses the mistakes made by Strunk & White)
- *A real dictionary*

Other recommendations for "writerly" reading

Ernest Hemingway thought that young writers (and by this, I mean writers new to the craft, regardless of how young) ought to read the following list of essential books:

- *Blue Hotel* by Stephen Crane
- *The Open Boat* by Stephen Crane
- *Madame Bovary* by Gustave Flaubert
- *Dubliners* by James Joyce
- *The Red and the Black* by Stendhal
- *Of Human Bondage* by Somerset Maugham
- *Anna Karenina* by Leo Tolstoy
- *War and Peace* by Leo Tolstoy
- *Buddenbrooks* by Thomas Mann
- *Hail and Farewell* by George Moore
- *The Brothers Karamazov* by Fyodor Dostoevsky
- *The Oxford Book of English Verse*
- *The Enormous Room* by E.E. Cummings
- *Wuthering Heights* by Emily Brontë
- *Far Away and Long Ago* by W.H. Hudson
- *The American* by Henry James

I must confess that I have read only two or three of Papa Hemingway's recommendations. My only explanation for this oversight is that I'm a work-in-progress—as any *bona fide* writer will always be.

As you can see, reading widely—cross-reading—does several things for a writer, from improving your writing to shaping your ideas. But what other methods can you use to develop those ideas once they're in your head?

Using journaling to shape your writing

And what about this journaling stuff? Do you keep journals? In my view, you should. I cannot imagine a writer who doesn't have at least several journals on the go at any time. The main reason for keeping a journal is that, above all else, it gives you a recurring opportunity to work on your writing—to shape your ideas—without the self-consciousness of knowing others will read it. Indeed, as I continue to suggest, not everything we write should be published (or even seen by others, but we'll get to that in a later chapter). Journal writing helps us to shape our ideas. As Susan Sontag once said: *"In the journal, I do not just express myself more openly than I could to any person; I create myself."*

I keep multiple journals. It seems I'm a tad addicted to the notion of journals. I have journals that require pen and paper, and journals that reside on my computer. As you can see, I'm not a purist either way.

Virginia Woolf once said, *"The habit of writing for my eye only is good practice,"* which sums up the first reason for keeping a journal. As I said before, it gives you a chance to work on your writing without the self-consciousness of knowing others will read it. Although this might, at first glance, seem like I'm referring to the cathartic kind of journaling that has become the ubiquitous habit of the navel-gazers among us, it's more than that. This kind of journaling is an exercise that lets you try out different turns of phrase and permits your mind to wander to ideas deeply buried in your subconscious. It is also a safe place for writing that you have no intention of showing anyone else. And this kind of journaling can be semi-structured.

Writer and teacher Natalie Goldberg (whose work I mentioned at the beginning of this chapter) takes a unique approach to journaling, a method I've come back to year after year. In her first writing book, *Writing Down the Bones* (initially published in 1986, with a twenty-fifth-anniversary edition published in 2016), she suggests that you take pen to paper—a real pen or pencil to real paper. She is adamant about this—placing your pen on the paper, keeping it moving and never lifting it for your ten-minute writing practice each day. Her rule is inflexible: keep your hand moving. Begin with the words "I remember..." or even "I don't remember..." whenever you get stuck. (She has other suggestions, but you'll have to read her book to get those.) Never stop or lift the pen as it moves across the page. Every time your hand begins to hesitate, write "I remember..." again and keep going for the full ten minutes. Try it. Right now. It's a very liberating process.

There are reasons other than practice for keeping journals, though. One of my primary motivations is to have places to store ideas that come to me. These ideas can be thoughts, clippings, photos, etc. However, I also have general-idea journals and a special journal for every project I'm working on. Okay, I have lots of journals, but I'd wager a guess that I'm not the only one!

One of the journals I kept for many years was a bit like a diary, but it focused on only one of the general kinds of experiences in my life. It chronicled my experience as a ballet mom. That journal became the basis for my memoir, *Another 'Pointe' of View: The Life and Times of a Ballet Mom*. There, I wrote about my day-to-day experiences of having a child away from home to attend an elite, professional ballet school from the age of eleven so that he could pursue his talent and his dream. It also allowed me to explore how I felt about this in general—the role of the parent with a gifted child and the peculiarities of this elite school in particular. I was able to capture detailed memories that would have faded into the mists of my mind, which would have been altered by subsequent experiences when I tried to retrieve them later. That journal was critical to my ability to write a story that might resonate with other parents of artistically gifted children.

Right now, as always, I have many journals on the go. I have two that hold notes on two separate book projects. I have one that is a kind of general catch-all for ideas. I have a travel journal. I have one full one that kept notes about a book that my husband wanted to write in his retirement. I have a journal full of notes I made as I wrote a recently published book. So, should I throw away the notes now? Probably. I also have two new, blank journals that have not yet found their purpose, but they will eventually and the fact that they are empty speaks of many possibilities. I love that feeling. I also have two computer-based journals and one on my iPad.

The best part of my journals, though, is when I look into one of them, and what I read becomes part of something larger—something I'll write that someone else might read and enjoy—or at least learn from. That's a great feeling.

Paper or digital? Which journal is best for you?

Do you ever write with a pen and paper? Honestly? Or are you forever hunched over the computer keyboard like most writers these days? If you only ever write on a computer keyboard, I think you might be missing out on something. Stay with me for a few moments, all you tweeters.

Some people think that writing creative pieces needs to be done by putting pen to paper—literally.

Ever since I discovered her work in the late 1980s, I have considered Natalie Goldberg among my principal writing teachers. I've never met Ms. Goldberg. My writing is not one bit like her writing, but her early books on writing practice were my signposts along the journey toward finding my voice as a writer. Although I'm seriously dedicated to writing while hunched over a keyboard, Natalie's approach to teaching writing has often given me pause. It forced me to consider whether there is a difference in the extent to which we can mine our creativity when entering words into a computer versus letting them flow onto paper through our writing hand.

Natalie's approach to writing, as I mentioned, is that it is a *practice* and that by practicing, we improve our writing. We don't have to publish everything we write. Writing is often for ourselves only and should remain private, as I continue to repeat. To tell you the truth, I often read material that I wish the writer *had* kept to him or herself!

She tells us to *"lose control."* This is easier said than done, but I believe this is how we mine our creativity. As writers, we put pen to paper, and if we're able to lose control and keep the writing hand moving, interesting ideas just seem to flow. There is some scientific evidence to support the benefits of putting pen to paper.

Research on the differences between handwriting and computer-writing suggests that handwriting has a few advantages that can help writers. First, writing with a pen and paper seems to improve recall. This means that all those students in university classrooms these days tapping away at their tablets and laptops may have a more challenging time remembering important information than their counterparts taking hand-written class notes. Other research supports the notion that writing by hand improves our focus. Wouldn't it be nice to feel that you are focusing on your writing while you're doing it? I am not suggesting that we all give up our keyboards. That would be the death of my writing career. I'm suggesting that if we all took the time to *write by hand from time to time*, we might see our writing differently.

In a helpful piece on *The Guardian*'s book blog, Lee Rourke wrote about the benefits of creative writing via the pen. He referred to longhand writing as a "secretive pleasure." He says he "…can sit in a corner of a café unnoticed and write to my heart's content. I'm less conspicuous than the iBook brigade, cluttering up London coffee houses and pubs with their flashy technologies."

Of course, my obsession with writing journals is related to the notion of putting pen to paper. Sometimes, it's just pleasant to sit in a comfortable chair and think. Then, pick up that journal and just write. I will admit that I often pick up my iPad and do this these days, but to tell you the truth, it's not the same. I highly recommend a good dose of the Natalie Goldberg approach to writing practice—with that pen firmly planted on a piece of paper that (preferably) is contained in a beautiful notebook.

Reading and journaling may be two good ways to begin to shape your writing, but how do you then practice it so that it improves? On to the next chapter.

EIGHT

Ideas for Your Writing Practice

"To write is human, to edit is divine." ~ Stephen King

JUST LIKE ATHLETES AND DANCERS, those of us who call ourselves writers need to *practice* our craft and *warm up* before embarking on a new piece of work.

Whenever I'm faced with the prospect of a brand-new writing project and find myself sitting in front of that blank computer screen, fingers poised over the keys, I need to feel that I am in practice and that I'm warmed up to begin properly. So, how do writers practice writing when they're not writing something destined for publication in one way or another? How do we warm up for the task at hand?

As we discovered in the previous chapter, writers' journals are bedrock tools for shaping ideas. They are also obviously useful for writing practice, and you'll want to use them for that. However, keeping journals is not the only way to practice your writing—and you must practice.

Blogging as writing practice

We begin by casting our minds back to when blogging started in 1998, when these "weblogs," as they were initially called, appeared online to provide online journals—so there's a direct relationship between journaling and blogs—although one is private, the other can be public. In a sense, *a blog is a journal gone public*. Although, to be clear, even a blog can be kept private – and often ought to be. More about that later.

Like everyone else, I started a blog when blogging first became a force to be reckoned with. I thought I could use the blog to make some of the work I do at the university available to a broader audience – but I wasn't committed to it. As I look back on the exercise now, I think I wanted to learn the technical aspects of blogging more than I wanted it to be good pieces of writing. But blogging can be the practice space that writers need.

Consider this: if you are a writer, you need to write every day—or at least those five days a week that you devote to "work." (I know, some of your friends don't think you're really working when all you seem to be doing is sitting at home diddling away on the computer—my mother thinks that if I'm not in front of a class or at a meeting, I must not be working. I wonder where she thinks those books come from?) But you don't always have a big project—and sometimes, when you do, all you seem to be able to do is stare at that blank screen. This situation is where blogging as a writing practice comes in.

Blogging, however, can only be a practice if you are committed to it. Being committed means committing to writing almost every day and posting at least every week or two if your blog is for public consumption. But do you *have* to make every blogged thought available to the masses? In a word, NO!

Not every blog has, or needs, an audience. Believe it or not, you can blog away with your settings set to private. It does not need to be searchable by the Googles of the world. It does not need tags or keywords.

For most people, blogging requires an idea that triggers a personal response, which becomes the basis for a blog post that begs for a reader's response. Blogging, in this scenario, is a very public activity that begs for that dialogue. Blogging as writing practice, on the other hand, does not need an idea or an angle. It does not require an audience and certainly doesn't need any feedback. It just needs the writer to begin with a word or two—such as "I remember …" an approach we've already discussed—and fingers to the keyboard, repeating those two words every time the ideas stop flowing. What's very important here is that what you write doesn't even have to be good—it just has to *be*. Unless, of course, you make it public. Then it does have to be good. Your reputation as a writer is at stake.

This is how I justify spending time on my blogs—my husband and I also blog about our other passion—travel. My blogs began as ways simply to practice and warm up before a big project. They have evolved. The nice thing about writing practice (even in your journals) is that you never know where it might lead. They just don't need to have an objective at the outset.

Blogs might be the news sources of the twenty-first century for many people, but blogging can be so much more for writers. However, you'll receive a different message from some people in the online writing communities. Some online writers consider blogging to be a complete waste of your time. The naysayers are trying to make the point that blogging wastes time by serving both a relatively small blog audience and the audience you are trying to cultivate for your books. I'm suggesting that using blogging as a writing practice, rather than seeing it as a way to serve and gather readers for your book, is the way forward for the unknown writer. Once you are no longer an anonymous writer but a known writer with your own fans, you can decide whether you want to spend time writing for them on a more periodic basis, which is the blog's fundamental approach. Use your blog to practice.

What blogging can accomplish for your writing

A private blog can be such a gift to yourself. A public blog can be a gift for you and for others. Now let's focus on public blogs as writing tools.

Here are some things you can accomplish with a blog:

- By setting a blogging schedule for yourself, you can practice keeping a writing momentum. In the next chapter, we'll discuss goals and deadlines further.
- Sometimes, you have ideas you'd like to explore but don't fit in with your current writing projects. Your blog is a great space for these ideas.
- You can practice your self-editing skills. We can all benefit from more of this.
- You can get feedback from readers if that's what you're looking for, but remember, writing with a view to other people reading it is very different from the freedom that comes from writing for your eyes only.

Other writing practice approaches

There are also other ways to practice your writing. One that might resonate with you is using *writing prompts*. A writing prompt is no more than a word, a phrase, or a paragraph that you use to kick-start your creative process. Some people use prompts to deal with slow periods in their writing on a specific project. I suggest that you consider using them for free writing simply to practise your craft regularly. But where do you get prompts?

First, there are online writers' services websites that provide such prompts. Here are a few places to start:

- Writer's Digest Creative Writing Prompts: http://www.writersdigest.com/prompts
- 400+ Creative Writing Prompts to Find Your Next (Best) Book Idea: https://self-publishingschool.com/fiction-creative-writing-prompts/
- Reedsy Prompts: https://blog.reedsy.com/creative-writing-prompts/
- 365 Creative Writing Prompts: https://thinkwritten.com/365-creative-writing-prompts/

Other sources for prompts for your writing practice can come from any of the following:

- Tweets in your news feed: People say the darnedest things in their tweets, and these can be a great source of writing practice prompts. You could also use news tweets.
- Pinterest boards: Searching through quotation pictures on Pinterest will net you many writing practice starters.
- Quotation sites such as Brainy Quote (http://www.brainyquote.com/), The Quote Garden (http://www.quotegarden.com/) and Quoteland (http://www.quoteland.com/).
- On Twitter follow @writingprompts, @writingprompt, @pictureprompts and @dailyprompt.

Finally, you can follow *Moonlight Press* on YouTube for an even more interesting approach to the writing prompt. They have a series of "Inspiration Snips," micro-mini movies that provide sights, sounds, and atmosphere, along with a voice-over story starter. You can subscribe by searching for Moonlight Press on YouTube.

In the next chapter, we'll talk about how you can discipline yourself to practise regularly.

NINE

Deadlines, Schedules and Momentum

"I love deadlines. I love the whooshing noise they make as they go by." ~ Douglas Adams

WRITING REQUIRES HARD WORK to get it right and demands self-discipline to get to the finish line. Successful, productive writers are, in equal measure, talented, inspired and disciplined. Arguably, they may even be more disciplined than inspired or even talented. That's how important it is to learn to be self-motivated and efficient.

Not long ago, I picked up a book that I didn't initially realize was really about the dreaded deadline. Okay, I now realize that Chris Baty's entertaining little book *No Plot? No Problem* isn't supposed to be about deadlines, but it is. Baty, the creator of the National Novel Writing Month (NaNoWriMo for those in the know), says this in the first chapter:

> *"Deadlines are the dynamos of the modern age. They've built every city, won every contest, and helped all of us to pay our taxes*

reasonably close to on time...a deadline is...optimism in its most ass-kicking form...a potent force..." (p. 26)

It occurs to me that I've been sympathetic to this point of view for many years. Just ask the students who populated my university classes for some twenty-six years. One thing I know for sure about writing is that you will never finish a writing project without self-discipline.

What it means to be disciplined

Of all the most narcissistic life pursuits, writing may well be near the top of the list. After all, you are not answerable to anyone but yourself. No one will criticize you for showing up late or not showing up at all. But you will have to face yourself. And eventually, you may even have to meet a contracted deadline.

The truth is that when it comes to your writing, it is yours and yours alone. From time to time, you might be given an external point of reference, such as a contracted deadline—which we'll get to—but even then, discipline for a writer means self-discipline. You have to build and maintain momentum to reach that deadline.

Self-control. Self-restraint. Willpower. Regardless of what you call it, the concept is clear for your writing life: you need to be in control of your writing and motivate yourself to complete projects. No one will do it for you.

How deadlines organize our writing

A deadline changes everything about any project that you plan to implement. It moves you past the planning stage and drops you headfirst into the implementation phase, forcing you to consider milestones along the way. And when an external force (like your boss or your professor or your editor) imposes a deadline, those deadlines take on even greater importance. Or do they?

Although some writers focus on one writing project at a time, I always have several writing projects on the go simultaneously. For many years, one of those projects was always academic, but as I moved through that phase of my life, those writing projects gradually dropped down the priority list. These days, I will generally have two writing projects going at once—one will be a nonfiction piece, the other a novel. And, of course, I also help other writers along the way, a pursuit that I love. Each individual project feeds off the other, but somewhere along the line, I need to ensure that one or more projects actually make it to the finish line. For that to happen, I need to be organized and disciplined. And I need to do it myself.

For example, one personal project I completed regularly during its heyday was my contribution to the travel blog I have written with my husband for many years, as I've mentioned. Why? Because I had a *self-imposed deadline*. I made a personal commitment to a certain number of posts at specific intervals when we started this, and I have rarely missed my deadlines since. That isn't to say that we haven't changed the schedule over the years of keeping that blog. We certainly have. In any case, I am proud to say I have *never* missed an externally-imposed writing deadline, which has shocked almost every publisher I have ever worked with, especially academic presses. It also occurs to me that when I have taken the time to *create personal deadlines*, my work has progressed faster and more efficiently than using the more organic, artistic approach to work schedules that seems to be common among many of the "creatives" of the world.

Here is a case in point. Some years ago, I decided to take a foray into screenwriting. I think it's because I see plot and dialogue as a kind of film running through my head when I write narrative, so I thought I might capitalize on that tendency. I registered for a script-writing course and set about learning the nuts and bolts of the process (not to mention learning about the paranoia that seems to run rampant through the film industry: no one wanted to share their ideas for fear of them being stolen—this never seems to happen in the world of books). After I completed the course, I had a script framework, ideas and scraps of dialogue, but not much else. So, I did what I always do: I bought a book on script-writing.

In fact, I bought several, but the one that took me to a different level is not Robert McKee's classic (and excellent) book, *Story*; instead, it is a small book called *How to Write a Movie in 21 Days* by Viki King. I followed her framework for getting to a finished ninety-minute script in twenty-one days, and it worked. I have the proof of it sitting in a file drawer, just waiting for a producer/director to snatch it up. But I had not noticed that her admonitions about deadlines got inside my head. She says, "…your deadline…is your friend. Focus on reaching your deadline. Make it your priority. Sleep, food and phone are secondary to the deadline…"

We need to keep in mind that this was published in 1993. These days, King would have had to add a list of social networking sites to avoid while focusing on your deadline.

The bottom line is that if I impose a deadline on myself, I get it done. This merely means writing and not stopping to try to get everything perfect. Just get the project finished. There will always be time for editing later—with an editing deadline, of course!

From a slightly different perspective, novelist Rita Mae Brown offers us this about deadlines: "*A deadline is negative inspiration. Still, it's better than no inspiration at all.*"

Word-count schedules

There's an ongoing meme about writing 1000 words a day in the online writing communities. Or it used to be. These days, I see admonitions to write 5000 words a day. Why 1000? Why 5000? I'm not sure where this originated, but in my own writing life, I've been doing this for many years, when working on a long-form project I really would like to see finished: I set a daily word count. And here's the key to developing your word-count schedule. Do you really want to complete the project? As we discussed in the previous two chapters, if it's just writing practice, you can just as easily use a journal or a blog with no word count schedule. But if you have a longer project, like a book you want to finish, you need to think about some kind of schedule. Word count is probably the best place to begin.

This kind of schedule has become so intertwined in the online writers' culture that there are even software packages to help these days. According to wordcounter.net, Mark Twain produced 1400-1800 words a day, Stephen King 2000 a day, Hemingway 500, Jack London 150, Nicholas Sparks 2000, Anne Rice (one of my personal favourites) 3000 a day, and the late Michael Crichton (another of my favourites) a whopping 10,000 words a day! However, it's interesting to note that authors like the late Arthur Hailey, whose novels were often lengthy, wrote only 600 words a day, and Tom Wolfe, author of *The Right Stuff* and *The Bonfire of the Vanities*, evidently produced a mere 135. Note, however, that it took him eleven years to finish one of his 370,000-word books. So, you can see that there is quite a range. It is a myth that you have to write a certain number of words a day. But you do have to write something.

However, the problem with this is that I can never be sure how long the finished product will be. And this piece of information would be helpful in setting word-count goals. For example, a piece of historical fiction might be 80,000 words, but the story might take me 100,000. This either means that the story is just that long, or, and perhaps this is more often the case, the story is *too* long—it is too wordy. In this latter situation, what it needed is a severe and substantive edit. Figuring out how long a piece of writing ought to run is the challenge.

There are accepted standards, but beginning writers often point to much longer (or shorter) published works in their genres to support the notion of what sells in their categories. Chuck Sambuchino, writing on the *Writer's Digest blog* (which I recommend), has this response: "Almost always, high word count means that the writer simply did not edit their [sic] work down enough." Over the years, I restricted my writing to certain times of day, working around my work responsibilities and my less predictable family responsibilities. As a result, I picked a random 1000 words for each writing day, projecting how many words I could then, realistically, produce in a month. It has always provided me with a certain amount of momentum, for sure. I've recently increased my goal to 2000 words a day with the caveat that it is a soft goal. I often write more.

For a bit of counterpoint, though, it's worth mentioning that not all writers are as enamoured of the word-count goals as I appear to be. One writer-blogger, for example, suggests that they can be destructive. She warns writers that focusing on word count rather than the work can be damaging to the writing itself. I think this is a valid point. For her, using a time schedule was more productive. This approach strikes me as a good alternative for those who become too focused on that word count—a cautionary tale.

Increasing your daily word count

Once you have developed your momentum for writing regularly, you might toy with the idea of increasing that daily goal. It's a bit like weight-training specific muscle groups: eventually, the lighter weight becomes too easy. You need more of a challenge (remember Anne Rice and Michael Crichton for a bit of inspiration), and you'll accomplish more in the process. But how can you do this?

First, harken back to our discussion about pre-planning your work. If you create a ***plan or proposal*** for yourself before you begin a writing project, you are more likely to be able to push through to a new word-count level. You don't have to spend time figuring out your direction; you can simply write. I write plans of varying complexity for just about everything I write. As the writing gains momentum, the plan becomes less and less important. Whenever I lose that forward motion, though, I can go back to the plan to see where it can take me next. The final product might only slightly resemble the original plan, but the plan kept me going.

Do as much of the *research* as you can before you begin. Although you might think that only nonfiction writers need to research their work before embarking on it, even fiction writers of both literary and genre fiction need to do research. Obviously, if you're writing historical fiction, for example, there is an enormous amount of pre-research that you can do and frankly need to do before you write even a single word. Other genres, however, also require research, a situation that I discussed earlier in the book. And make no mistake, even if you write contemporary literary fiction, there are pieces of research you need to do. Here are some examples of the kinds of research materials that will provide the background details you need and stimulate ideas that you may have never considered.

- *Setting*: cities, streets, buildings, plants and landscapes, weather, political environment, and economic situation.
- *Characters*: behaviours, physical characteristics (e.g., birth defects, racial features, psychological types), personality traits.
- *Storyline*: Answers to questions like the following: *Will this mode kill a person immediately? What happens when someone is stabbed with this implement in this part of the body?* I recently read an excerpt from a self-published title where the main character was brutally stabbed in the first three pages, the type of injuries that were not compatible with continued life. Indeed, if the attack were to be believed as portrayed, the woman would have been dead, thereby effectively ending her story before it began. (I know this because it was excruciatingly obvious, but I got corroboration from a physician—my husband.) However, she dragged herself upright and presumably romped through the rest of the book. Basic research would have told the author that the woman could not still be alive (no, this was not a vampire story, a mummy story or any other story about the living dead or someone with super-human characteristics). I had to stop reading because it was clear the author had done no research to determine how far the attack could go before the character should die. I cannot read a book where the author fails to do even a modicum of background research. Most other readers won't accept it either.

Realistically, the bottom line is that you'll have to **devote more time** to your writing to increase your productivity. This means keeping track of how long it takes you, on average, to write those

1000 (or 500 or 5000) words. You can then increase the time commitment to the same level as the new word count. If it takes you, on average, two hours to write 1000 words, and you'd like to increase that to 1500 words per day, you will have to schedule three hours. It's a simple mathematical formula. If your math isn't particularly good, you'll have to trust me on this and use a computer to figure out your own numbers.

Word count and time goals are beneficial, but they are not the only ways to enhance your productivity. You'll need momentum.

Writer's block and momentum

There can't be a writer among us who hasn't heard of writer's block. It's the greatest excuse for procrastination that you can use as a writer. There are two questions that you need to answer. First, is there really any such thing as writer's block? Second, is it really a block or just a temporary delay in your writing, and how do you overcome it? Let's first deal with the question of whether there is such a thing.

Writer's block is generally agreed to be any situation in which a writer cannot seem to start, continue or finish a piece of writing. But there are different kinds of writer's block. It could be one of the following:

- Not being able to come up with a new idea.
- Not knowing where your ideas are going.
- Not being able to figure out how to end a story.
- You're bored with the piece you're writing.

It does seem that most well-known, successful writers acknowledge that some kind of writer's block does exist. As Anne

Lamott (whose work I recommended to you earlier in this book) wrote in her book *Bird by Bird: Some Instructions on Writing and Life*, "Writer's block is going to happen to you. You will read what little you've written lately and see with absolute clarity that it is total dog shit..." or your writing comes to a complete halt, or you aren't writing at all. This is writer's block, and you need to do something about it if you're determined to recover your momentum.

Many people have lots of advice on what to do about these situations. I'm going to give you a few ideas, but first, let me tell you what I believe to be the most important thing to do to *prevent* writer's block (which, in my view, is far preferable to having to deal with it). My approach is to always have more than one writing project on the go at once (as previously noted).

Working on more than one project at a time might seem a bit counter-intuitive to the idea of staying focused. However, when you lose momentum on one project, you can move to the other one, which often energizes and stimulates ideas for the first (keep a notebook on each project).

Some other ideas include the following:

- Free write in one of your journals. Just keep writing.
- Write two to three pages of absolute crap in the book you're working on and then get rid of it later. Just keep writing.
- Use a writing prompt to kick-start your brain.
- Cross-pollinate your creativity by doing some other creative activity like sketching, painting or designing a dress.

Or perhaps you can do as Mark Twain once suggested:

> *"The secret of getting ahead is getting started. The secret of getting started is breaking your complex, overwhelming tasks into small, manageable tasks, and then starting on the first one."*

How to use 'found' time

For someone like me, who has spent decades as a university professor, there was a little perk I could take advantage of every three to five years. It's called a sabbatical. It's funny how people respond when you tell them you're on sabbatical. They usually say something like, "Gee, must be nice." (With just that slight edge of sarcasm.) Or they might say, "You university people have all the perks." Well, let's just say that few people would not have liked to be in my shoes when I was on sabbatical, regardless of how much they like their jobs. For others not quite as fortunate, having a sabbatical might mean taking time off work (paid or unpaid) or just finding that extra time you didn't expect, like when your in-laws unexpectedly cancel the family reunion weekend. However, for any writer who finds him or herself in this wonderful situation or with any unexpected gift of time, the question becomes how to best spend that "found time."

So, what's a sabbatical anyway? Naturally, the web is full of definitions. Let's start with the etymology of the word (where an English word has its source).

The word derives from and is related to a bunch of words in other languages. The Latin *sabbaticus*, the Greek *sabbaitkos*, and even the Hebrew *Shabbat* all have similar meanings. They refer to a hiatus from work. This is interesting to a university professor, I'm sure, since a sabbatical always meant a break from my regular teaching and administrative responsibilities, but the requirement to produce work related to the other components of a professor's contract is even higher. Those other components are, of course, research and writing. A university professor on sabbatical is supposed to be researching and writing, not sitting around eating potato chips and catching up on Netflix. The idea, though, that one can be freed up from other daily responsibilities to focus more fully on the kind of work that really is done better with single-minded focus from time to time, is a forward-thinking one. Everyone should have a sabbatical occasionally. But not to lie around slothfully and vegetate, in my view. So, what kind of productive work can a writer produce when she is on sabbatical from other work?

The following are my four tips to make the best use of your found time:

1) *Be realistic about your time availability.* How much time can you really contribute to your writing? Even found time often competes with other demands.
2) *Structure your writing time.* As much as it might seem that this is a chance to live that creative life (i.e., the *perception* that writers go for coffee, work out at the gym, catch up on their reading and wait for the muse to strike), that kind of creative life is one of the myths of the writing life. Writing requires discipline, and discipline requires structure. Make a schedule for the following:
    a. The number of words you'd like to write in a day or a session.
    b. The amount of time you'd like to spend on preparation for writing.
    c. How long you will need to do the required research for your writing.

To tell you the truth, this is a no-brainer for me. I think that if you can't even make a date with yourself to write, then you'll never get a project finished, especially when you have so much more freedom than usual.

3) *Plan to reward yourself for accomplishing the above.* Rewards are great, but you also need to revisit tip #1 to ensure that your goals are realistic. You also need to assure yourself that this represents more than the very minimum you could accomplish. I can write thousands of words a day, but that doesn't mean they will be the words I should write. On the other hand, if I were to set my goal for 500 words a day and then went out for lunch as a reward, not only would I be under-performing, but I'd also probably be fat!

4) *Develop a writing ritual.* You'd be surprised how many creative people suggest this. Twyla Tharp, world-renowned choreographer and author of *The Creative Habit* (which I recommend you read from time to time), says, "It's vital to establish some rituals—automatic but decisive patterns of behaviour—at the beginning of the creative process when you are most at peril of turning back…Turning something into a ritual eliminates the question, why am I doing this?" She then provides numerous examples of artists' rituals. For example, Igor Stravinsky evidently always did the same thing every morning as he entered his studio: He sat down and played a Fugue by Bach. Then he got to work. We're more likely to check email or Twitter these days, but I don't recommend that as your ritual. It can precipitate a whole lot of trouble as the act itself begins to consume ever-larger portions of your day. I suggest leaving the online

rituals until later. Perhaps make them the reward! (see #3 above)

If you happen to be lucky enough to find yourself with some unexpected free time, you might want to consider putting it to good use to finish that writing project. Getting to the finish line by using your time well and creating your own momentum is exhilarating. And when you have all this time to yourself, you can be very productive. But will your writing time always be spent in solitary activity? It's now time to explore your non-solitary time.

TEN

Other People: Is There Safety in Numbers?

"A collection of a hundred great brains makes one big fathead."
Carl Gustav Jung

IT'S OFTEN BEEN SAID THAT WRITING is a solitary occupation. Franz Kafka opined as much when he wrote: *"Writing is utter solitude, the descent into the cold abyss of oneself."* My approach to writing is, in fact, very private. I rarely let others read my unfinished work. And only under specific circumstances have I ever actually written with a co-author, and it has been a very specific co-author.

The only person who regularly reads my work-in-progress is my trusty in-house editor and occasional collaborator, my husband. I have never been a personal fan of writing groups. But these days, it is next to impossible to avoid that kind of inter-author engagement altogether, given the plethora of social media and perhaps even the necessity for developing what has become that annoying phrase: the writer's platform, which we'll dive into in much greater detail in the final section of this book.

As we discuss this issue, perhaps it might be a good idea to keep in mind two differing perspectives. Henry Ford's view was summarized when he opined: *"Coming together is a beginning; keeping together is progress; working together is success."* We would also do well to remember what Scott Adams, the creator of the *Dilbert* cartoons, said: *"Few things in life are less efficient than a group of people trying to write a sentence. The advantage of this method is that you end up with something for which you will not be personally blamed."* Clearly, producing automobiles is much more conducive to teamwork than writing is. I happen to believe that this is true.

This begs a couple of questions for general discussion: Do writers need other people? And if they do, what do they need them for?

To collaborate or not to collaborate?

They say that there is strength in numbers, but is there really? Suppose you read a curriculum vitae (CV: an academic résumé) of just about any academic you can think of (but it's not reading I recommend unless you're an insomniac). In that case, you'll probably be surprised at how many of the books and papers they list as their accomplishments are penned by groups—occasionally, rather large groups. My own publication list on my academic CV is probably shorter than some, but my list of publications is just that—mine. No one else got tenured or promoted based on the same list of publications. As I said, they're mine—single-authored.

A university colleague once suggested that I form a committee to work on a report my department had tasked me with. I told this colleague the following: "I don't play well with others." And the very notion of writing a report by committee—well, let's just say that I value my time and sanity, and the amount of both it would take for me to make nice with the collaborators is not worth the effort usually.

If you were to peer very closely at the descriptions of four of my past books, though, you will, in fact, see that I have, on those occasions, worked with someone else. Those are the exceptional circumstances I mentioned. That someone I have worked with from time to time was my husband, and we're still married. So, you see, it *can* work. I have "collaborated" on four nonfiction books on topics in which he and I share a certain amount of expertise (we have also installed foil wallpaper together and are still married). So, when is a writing collaboration a good idea?

Before you jump to the conclusion that collaborative writing works only in nonfiction, there have, in fact, been novels penned by duos (think: Emma Mclaughlin and Nicola Kraus of *Nanny Diaries* fame). However, the co-authors' names are sometimes combined into a single name so that the reader thinks the book has a single author. Consider the husband-and-wife team Judith Barnard and Michael Fain, who began their writing collaboration by writing feature articles for women's magazines and then began producing bestsellers under the pen name Judith Michael. If you browse through an online bookstore in the nonfiction sections, you'll see plenty of co-authored books. Then, if you scan a textbook site, you'll see an even higher percentage.

There are good reasons to collaborate and publish a co-authored book, such as when the knowledge and skills of more than just you are needed. And I begin with that notion of the collaborative "good idea" for a book.

Every book starts with an idea. Does a co-authored book originate in the mind of only one of the authors (in which case it will always be her baby, and she'll feel that sense of ownership), or does it come about as a double brainwave? I can only answer this in my case.

It all started in the very earliest years of our marriage when my husband and I used to go out every Friday night. It was nothing fancy; it was just a chef's salad and a carafe of house wine at a harbourfront watering hole. But sitting there, gazing out the window at the harbour lights, sipping a glass of mediocre wine that tasted like the finest French vintage at the end of a long week engendered in us a kind of romantic notion of leaving a legacy. What better way, we thought, than to write a book together. We had compatible—if not equivalent—backgrounds. I had a graduate degree in health education/communication, and he was a physician. Surely there was a common ground we could explore together. When we hit upon the idea, it was a *Eureka*! Moment—a collaborative one. I can honestly say that neither of us owned the idea.

For ten years, my husband had been the chairman of the Canadian Medical Association Ethics Committee, a post he vacated shortly after we married. A high-profile position involving extensive media coverage, the chairmanship required specific expertise and experience, which he had. For my part, I had studied ethics and written about ethics in health care as a medical writer. Since he had left his position as chairman, he was no longer required to toe the party line, as it were. It was a golden opportunity. We had the notion that we would be the ones to simplify complex ethical issues in health care for everyone. The public would be smitten, and they would see the wisdom in our ideas. At least that's the way we saw it at the time.

Ethics—healthcare ethics, to be specific—was, in fact, the subject of our first book. However, it didn't come together exactly as we had planned. You know the old saying: *if you want to make God laugh, just tell her your plans*. That was what sort of happened in our case.

As I have mentioned previously, I had developed successful book proposal writing skills, so I took charge of writing the proposal. We put our two perspectives on the topic together and mined our individual knowledge to develop what we thought was a well-rounded approach to helping the average, interested reader understand the ins and outs of ethical dilemmas in modern health care. At the same time, we decided that we could recycle the same research into another book aimed at a different audience (recycling your research is a strategy I highly recommend). Our idea was that we'd eventually write a textbook—an interdisciplinary textbook for all kinds of health professions students, and it would be a book that they would read. It would be unlike some of the ethics tomes we had to slog through as students. But our idea was to be sure that the book for the general public—the trade book—would be published first.

After pitching our ideas to suitable publishers for each of these different treatments of the subject, one small publisher in Toronto was interested in the textbook idea and offered us a contract. So, our book, *Healthcare Ethics*, with an audience focus *not* on the general public but on health professionals, was born.

Then the real work began. At least four evenings a week, after our young son had gone to bed, we'd hole up in our home office and work. We'd discuss the organization, content, references, and other aspects of the book. My husband, the doctor, kept notes each day as he saw patients in the office. We'd talk about each chunk of the book as a team, and then I'd write it. *I think that collaborations work best when you are clear about each person's skills and have a well-defined idea of the roles each will play.* It is a myth that both authors can be equally involved in all aspects of the project. That realization needs to begin with an honest assessment of your own skills. Our process developed as follows: I'd write, then the manuscript went back to him. He'd make copious and substantive notes, then I'd rewrite with his notes and mine. This process happened a few times for each chunk of the material until we had a completed draft.

In the end, the publisher was happy with the book, and we had found our writing rhythm. This publication was the first of four books we would write together. The most important lesson we learned is that *you must first really like and respect the person you're working with.* Second, *you must have a clear-eyed recognition of one another's knowledge and skills.* Then, and only then, would I recommend it as an approach to writing your book.

Independent or co-dependent? Writers & other strangers

The indie music scene? Now that's an image most of us can get our heads around. As Catherine Andrews wrote for CNN online a few years ago, "If it's cool, creative, and different, it's indie…" If, like me, you've been around writing and publishing for more than a few years, when you think about indie publishing, you probably don't get the same vibe—or perhaps you didn't, until very recently. I, for one, would really like to, though. Let's start with the word itself: What precisely does the word *independent* mean?

I like to start with a dictionary. According to the Oxford English Dictionary online, *independent* means the following: "Free from outside control; not subject to another's authority." That sounds just about right. The dictionary also suggests that the word means "…not depending on another for livelihood or subsistence," and my personal favourite, "…capable of thinking or acting for oneself." So indie writers should be self-sufficient, self-supporting and autonomous.

The Alliance of Independent Authors (AIA) suggests that there is even more to being an "indie" *author*. An author is one step beyond being a writer, but the AIA perspective is interesting in this discussion. According to their website, an indie author meets the following criteria:

1) Has self-published at least one book. (Note that they rightly indicate that you are not an author unless you are published. On the other hand, you need not have published to be a so-called writer.)
2) Is the "creative director" of all his or her own publishing projects from the beginning to the end of the process. (This is what self-publishing is all about, so they may have conflated self-publishing with indie, and I'm not convinced they are the same thing. I believe indie is broader than simply self-publishing.)
3) Is the "creative director" of an author's business. (Others have coined the god-awful term *authorpreneur*.)
4) Is proud of being an indie author. (The fact that they have to say this suggests a kind of chip-on-the-shoulder mentality that it's time everyone got over. Indie music scene, anyone?)

However, if we go back to the definition of independent, it seems that if you are truly indie, you also need to be unconstrained by others' thinking. You would do your own thing, so to speak. Is this really true?

In recent years, most of us, unknown writers, have begun spending more time on social networks frequented by readers and other writers. I have noticed an important phenomenon as I connect with so-called writers' communities online. **Writers are, by and large, more connected with other writers than they are with mentors or readers.** And it has puzzled me quite a bit that I am sometimes followed on Twitter by tweeters who have thousands of followers. Here's an illustration.

One day, I received a Twitter notification indicating that I had several new followers. My usual habit is to click over to their profiles to see if they would be people whose tweets might be interesting and/or useful to me. I suspect that not many people are like me. Others seem to either (a) automatically follow those who follow them—a questionable exercise depending on your objective for being on Twitter at all, or (b) try to figure out if the new follower could be useful to them. In any case, on this day, one of my new followers boasted some 81,000 followers of his own! Wow! Impressive, right? This individual must have a lot to offer. Well, not so much, I found by reading his tweets. And to make matters worse, he followed 75,000 people or organizations. Why in the world would he choose to follow me? This is the key question when it comes to online writing connections. Even if I had something useful that he might be interested in, he would never, NEVER see it among his thousands of tweets that would come to him daily. I might be ridiculously naïve when it comes to the power of social media—but I don't think so.

I'm as aware as the next person that there is a lot of power in the viral tweet, but the truth is that only a minuscule number of tweets garner the kind of publicity that most writers are looking for. And it is impossible to *plan* on a tweet going viral.

Even all these years later, since social media has become as ubiquitous as computers, there has been some, but not much, research on what makes social media messages go viral. No one has yet published a good, well-constructed study on why a tweet goes viral, but there have been some studies on the attributes of viral videos, though the results are vague, to say the least. It seems that there are two important characteristics of viral videos: the emotional content of the video and the source. If you can provoke anger, disgust or starry-eyed love (think of all those cute-animal videos), they are more likely to go viral. If you are Gwyneth Paltrow, however, you can tweet about any mundane aspect of your life, from what you had for breakfast to the kind of toilet paper you use, and the Twitterverse will lap it up. This is not unlike the old markers for what makes something news: these would represent prominence (of the source) and impact. The more emotional impact a story has, the more it qualifies as news. And the more prominent the individuals involved in the story, the greater its newsworthiness. So, nothing is vastly different. But unless these are genuine characteristics of what you really want others to know about you and your work, your results on social media are not likely to be what you want to achieve.

So, if you are seeking a large following on a social media platform like Tiktok or Instagram, are you truly independent and unconstrained by the thinking of others? Or do others' perspectives and actions make you a lemming?

There is a big difference between independent and codependent, with a kind of continuum between the two extremes. However, "codependent" is how I characterize many of the relationships between and among writers on social networking platforms like Twitter and Facebook (to a lesser extent on LinkedIn, but it's there, especially in some of the groups). Codependency means relying on someone else for excessive amounts of emotional or psychological support. In the case of these codependent writers' groups, each member is codependent on all the others. Doesn't sound at all like "indie", does it? However, it does seem to define many of the online relationships in writers' communities, in my view.

Is it the case that most of us use specific social networking sites only because of what we think we can get from them? What would happen if we took a different view? *Ask not what a social network can do for me, but what I can do for this social network.* Wouldn't that change a lot of those me-tweets and Instagram selfies? Then maybe we'd all actually get something out of it anyway!

Perhaps being a cool, indie writer means you have to be the one to ask what you can do for your social networks, rather than the other way around.

Traditional writers' groups

Although, as I mentioned earlier in this chapter, I'm not a joiner in the traditional sense, and I have eschewed writers' groups almost exclusively over my career, that doesn't mean that they have no value—and that doesn't mean that others who are more social might not benefit from them in ways that I might not. Regardless of my opinion, I'd be remiss in my discussion of writers as a part of a larger whole if I didn't mention them. Let's begin by examining what writers' groups are *intended* to accomplish.

First, a writing group is, by definition, a group of like-minded people who seek mutual support for their writing ventures. Many online writing mentors suggest that beginning writers seek out and join writing groups. The odd thing about this is that many well-established writers loathe them and never once attended a writer's group meeting or a writers' conference. Writing coach Jennie Nash, writing a guest piece on Jane Friedman's excellent and long-running blog, suggests that they can be seriously dangerous. "Writing groups can cause fatal frustration, deep self-doubt, and sometimes years of wasted effort," she writes. She then goes on to identify some of the dangers—a perspective that I happen to share.

First, she suggests that no one is really honest, and no one wants honesty anyway. From my own observation of online writing groups, I can tell you that this is absolutely true. I have seen wannabe writers post work that is just short of illiterate, after which the responses are "Love this!" "Very nice." And even, "Fantastic! I love it!" None of this is helpful to a "writer" whose grasp of the English language is tenuous at best.

She also suggests that newbie writers who themselves are struggling are not the best judges of what's good. See my comments above. No honesty coupled with no skill, and what do you have? The blind leading the blind.

The following are some of my suggestions for the questions you need to answer honestly for yourself before you join a writers' group, either online or in person:

- What are your personal goals in joining the group? Honest critique? Writing tips? Moral support for creating momentum?
- What are the group's goals? Do they even have any? If not, walk away.
- If they have goals, are they compatible with yours? Will you achieve your objective?
- Do the members of the group produce the kind of writing that you are most interested in?
- Do they spend more time plugging their own books than interacting? If so, run, don't walk away.
- Is it more of a social group or a working group? Is this what you are looking for?
- Do they have rules or guidelines for giving and receiving critiques? Or does everyone just provide knee-jerk reactions?
- Do you see or hear any constructive criticism at all? If all the feedback consists of positive, supportive comments, it's a codependent group.
- Do the members appear to get along with and respect one another?

Others obviously support the notion of writers' groups. They submit that these groups can help you improve your writing process and style and that other writers will better understand you than mere mortals could. I'm not convinced that this is true. If you hang around wannabe writers who publish every piece of schlock they jot down in a word-processing document, I don't think that's anything to aspire to if you want to be a writer. The problem is that most writers' groups are populated with other writers who are just as unknown and just as inexperienced as you are. Worse, it may hold any number of writers who think they are better than you are but aren't. In this kind of situation, it might be better to call the group a "beta reader" group—a group that will provide you with feedback but not a lot of insight on writing *per se*. It is a myth that you must belong to a writers' group. It might be worthwhile to remember what John Irving once wrote about writers seeking critiques: *"It's my experience that very few writers, young or old, are really seeking advice when they give out their work to be read. They want support; they want someone to say, 'Good job.'"* Amen to that.

Writing support groups are not unlike cancer or diabetes support groups: they are groups of like-minded individuals who share a similar experience but who don't possess the expertise of a professional. Be careful.

ELEVEN

Don't Publish Everything You Write: The Question of Quality

"The first draft of anything is shit." ~ Ernest Hemingway

THERE'S AN OLD, WELL-WORN MAXIM that is often quoted in ethics discussions, and it applies equally well to us writers: Just because you *can* do something doesn't mean you *should*.

The problem that faces writers and would-be writers in the twenty-first century is that we can publish every bit of genius and garbage that we produce. And it needs to be said that we all create some (perhaps a lot of) garbage, but only a few among us produce works of genius. Most of us inhabit that place somewhere between those two extremes in our usual writing. So, we need to make some decisions. How do we decide what to and what should be seen by our eyes only?

The era of the self-published author has brought the question of quality to the forefront. If self-publishing is to be thought of as a legitimate route to authorship, then writers need to be held to the same standards and measured by the same yardsticks as those published via the more traditional routes (see more about publishing terminology in the next chapter). In these days of "everyone is a writer" and "everyone is a publisher," we need some quality controls, and if writers themselves are not prepared to do this, then writing and publishing is doomed to mediocrity or worse.

I share my experiences with writing, publishing, buying, and reading (or trying to read) self-published and traditionally published titles, and offer suggestions for taming your desire to publish everything you write. Finally, the issue of the grammar-challenged provides a story and context for exploring quality issues. Grammar is only one of the quality considerations in your writing, but it is a good example of how you can go horribly wrong without realizing it.

Why you should not publish everything

After almost a quarter of a century of publishing experience—most via traditional publishers and recent indie experience topped up by more than one unsuccessful partnership with an agent—I realize that we writers should not publish everything. But sometimes, we need to face the truth a figure out how to tame ourselves.

Not everything you write is or even should be publishable. Discerning the difference between the publishable and the unpublishable takes honest and active scrutiny and a capacity to self-censor.

It is very liberating to know that what you are writing may be for your eyes only, and that's okay. Think about it: you have the luxury of time to write, and maybe it will be something that you'll share with the world. Knowing that it doesn't *have* to be shared can free you to write either better or worse than your norm. It doesn't matter.

Writing rubbish can be your writing practice. Just as a concert pianist does not usually have an audience for a practice session, you don't need (nor should you have) an audience for every word that makes it onto paper or your computer screen.

Get yourself a beta reader group if you absolutely need someone to read everything you write. Their feedback will almost certainly tame your desire to publish every word, but only if you choose readers who are not personal friends or want something from you in return. *Don't ask other writers*. You cannot expect honesty from them if they are codependent. If you frequent Facebook writers' groups, for example, you will find many offers from members who would be more than happy to be your beta readers. The problem is that they are also writers, and their independent opinions cannot be trusted.

If you insist on publishing every word that comes into your head, start a blog. And take pity on the rest of the world by keeping it private.

The truth is that there are far too many poorly written indie books out there, and this makes it harder for the fantastic indie writers to find their legitimate voice. Please do not protest that there are just as many traditionally published books full of errors and omissions. There simply are not. Editors see to that. Yes, the work may not be stellar storytelling in all cases, but it's been edited. I can't tell you how many times I've argued with editors, but in the end, their input has invariably improved my writing. And this goes for both my traditionally and independently published books.

And just like dancers need to warm up before a performance, make sure that you have a writing journal —for your eyes only, as we have discussed previously—that is the repository for those warm-up bits.

Holding writers to account for quality

One of the courses I taught throughout my academic career in communication was related to my original area of specialization in communication: namely health communication. I've written a lot in that area, including four or five books, all through traditional publishing channels. I developed the course to include a magazine health-feature writing assignment. It had been some years since I had done any medical feature writing myself at that time. As a result, I had to update my reference materials so that I might be able to offer the students a selection of current recommended resources. To that end, I began my book search where I usually begin: Amazon. To my surprise, the up-to-date offerings were slim.

As I made my way through the list in search of what might be a valuable book for my students, I came upon one titled *Popular Health & Medical Writing for Magazines*. I thought that sounded just like what the students might need, so I ordered a copy to review. I was remiss in my usual vetting of online book offerings.

I usually "look inside" to review the title page, table of contents, and copyright page and see who published it, then I check the author's bio to establish credentials. Then I read a few pages from the beginning of the book and search for a few phrases later on. I failed in my due diligence on this occasion.

Published by self-publishing behemoth iUniverse (a company with which I sadly have personal experience—a story I'll share in due course), the book turned out to be one of many (and I do mean many) books that this author has self-published. I'd be the last one to dismiss a book simply because it was self-published: many worthy books have been published by the authors themselves over the years, and I have some experience in it myself, as I've revealed. However, when I began to look closely at the credentials of this "popular science journalist" (as per the book description and her website, which I have unhappily subsequently perused), I was hard-pressed to find those credentials that would lead me to recommend her work.

Her other books include such things as books on how to write plays, monologues, or skits from life stories, social issues, current events for all ages, how to start personal history and genealogy journalism businesses, developing genealogy course templates, creating family newsletters and time capsules, and the list went on. There was even one about Middle Eastern honour killings in the USA (a novel, I believe, but I'm not sure), among many others. In fact, at the top of the author's website, it says that she has published 80 paperback books. This factor by itself should have been a big red flag if only I had visited her website before I bought the book instead of after. Indeed, what did this writer really know about popular health and medical writing? No one is an expert on such a dizzyingly wide range of subjects.

I have no quibble with writers having broad interests—I suffer from that myself; thus, I can identify—but I think there needs to be some area of expertise and solid credentials that can be identified if we look closely, especially in prescriptive nonfiction. Further, for someone to be writing a book about how to write health and medical pieces for popular media—well, let's just say that I expect to be able to see that they have a grasp both of medical science and journalism, as well as some experience in both. That was not evident—and I'm sad to report that the self-published book that I paid for was bewildering at best.

Why I didn't look at the first chapter title and get a clue is beyond me. The first chapter's title was "Making a medical language specialist: Turning medical transcribers into medical writers and editors." The notion that all you need to be a medical writer or editor is to have experience as a transcriptionist made me see red. Then sandwiched between a chapter titled "What to emphasize in medical writing…" and "Writing the self-help article" is a chapter titled "Writing about DNA and gene hunters." This made me begin to question both the framework and the book's agenda. Then the last chapter in this medical writing primer puzzled me even more: "Medical writing about pets: Care, food, travel, adventures, history, genres…" After spending several years in my early career doing medical writing, it had never once occurred to me—or to people buying my writing—that writing about the care and feeding—not to mention the adventures of one's pets—fell under the category of medical writing. It was news to me and another red flag that suggested the author was not, in fact, an expert of any kind.

So, I decided to read the book anyway. If I thought that the framework didn't make a lot of sense, the individual chapters had something of a flight of ideas as well. Then I came upon this piece of advice: "…medical writers can also sell (or represent) the product discussed in the research and writing…" That was the moment when I slammed the book shut, realizing that there was a severe shortage of ethical considerations among the pearls of wisdom. This conclusion led me to consider the following question: Should I write a review on Amazon to save other *bona fide* budding medical writers from buying this book? Or should I just let it go?

I felt that I didn't want to hurt the writer's feelings. Where did that thought come from? If self-publishing is ever to reach the level of a legitimate route to authorship, then writers need to be held to the same standards and measured by the same yardsticks as those published via the more traditional routes. I dropped the book into the paper recycling bin.

Clearly, the self-publishing model as it stands now needs some reconsideration. The problem is that the well-written and edited self-published books do hold their own against anything that a more traditional publisher can produce. Sadly, there is no way to figure this out unless you do what I did—and you buy it. By then, it's too late.

The belief that anyone can write (or should even consider writing) a book about any subject at all is preposterous. Just because you can do something doesn't mean you shouldn't take a long, hard look at your credentials and abilities. The overall lack of gatekeepers in the self-published universe is the single most problematic issue that threatens its long-term viability. Don't be the one to add another poorly written, deplorably edited, and disgustingly laid-out book to the scads of duds already out there.

Now to my one specific concern regarding the quality—or lack thereof—of books these days.

Grammar is important. Really

A few years ago, I was listening to the CBC (Canadian Broadcasting Corporation) noon-time call-in show on the radio as I drove from one appointment to another. The guest "expert" that day happened to be a grammar authority. I had missed the introduction, but I inferred from the ongoing discussion that he was a high school English teacher. He and the host discussed various aspects of grammar, and then listeners called in with their grammar-related questions and their pet peeves. In his attempt to avoid the jargon, as he put it, his explanations of why specific

English grammar rules are what they are lost something in the translation, making it difficult to view his explanations with much credibility.

Although grammar—which is the correct structure of our language—can be a part of the so-called style or voice of the writer, grammar is first and foremost a framework or structure for verbal and written communication in general. Grammatical mistakes frequently result in a failure to communicate, and so your message, whatever it may be, is lost. And besides, you must know the rules before you can break them.

A caller to the radio show guest asked him this simple question: *What is the difference in usage between 'bring' and 'take'?* It was his answer to this question that started to get me annoyed about the oversimplification of the rules.

His simplistic response was to tell her that "*I* bring" and "*You* take." I started thinking about this as the caller also tried to process this new information. I thought that this could not be right since *you* can also *bring* clarity to a situation (you wouldn't *take* clarity to a situation), and *I* can *take* action on something (I wouldn't *bring* action). His overly simplified rule is just wrong. Clearly, you can also decline both words: I bring, you bring, he brings etc.

Although messages can be the victim of the grammar-challenged among us, for me, it's often more of a simple stylistic issue. Most of the grammar mistakes that I find particularly annoying (somewhat like the sound of fingernails on a chalkboard in my world) are no more than personal pet peeves.

Some of our grammar-related pet peeves amount to nothing more than stylistic fads. For example, if I could just banish the word "impact" used as a verb, I think that I would have had an impact on (not impacted) style. That being said, it is now considered acceptable.

Aldous Huxley once wrote: "*A bad book is as much labour* [sic] *to write as a good one; it comes as sincerely from the author's soul.*" Quality and sincerity are two different things. Even when we have no quibble with the sincerity (although to be fair, in the twenty-first century, there is a lot of insincerity among the would-be writers seeking only to make money), many of us will indeed quibble with the quality of your published work. In the end, you will only be as successful as your last book.

Reality Check #3:

Talent is not Enough: Publishing is Hard Work

"Writing is like prostitution. First, you do it for love, and then for a few close friends, and then for money." ~ Molière

TWELVE

A Glossary for the 21st Century Writer

"Publishing is a business. Writing may be art, but publishing, when all is said and done, comes down to dollars."
~ Nicholas Sparks

ONE OF THE MOST IMPORTANT THINGS that any intelligent writer knows is this: *our words are our power*. This means we need a shared understanding of the words we use to convey the right messages. In the world of twenty-first-century publishing, confusion about jargon is common. In this chapter, I offer a glossary of terms to help you navigate the wild world of publishing. This will help us all have a shared understanding of the meanings of the terms we use. We'll explore many of these topics in more depth in the next few chapters to see how each relates to you and your work.

Author

Everything about publishing begins and ends with the author. Never let anyone lead you to believe differently. An author is someone who has published a book, article, paper, poem, report, etc. The act of publication distinguishes someone engaged in writing from an actual author. The method of publication does not matter.

Blurb

A book blurb is a short promotional paragraph, under 200 words, that captures the essence of a book. A blurb is the copy that appears on websites and on the back of physical books. Its purpose is to sell the book to the reader. For fiction, the blurb sets a mood and leaves a cliff-hanger so that the reader longs for more. For nonfiction, the blurb explains what the book is about and why readers should read it. A blurb is not a summary. Instead, it provides only enough information to captivate the reader.

Cooperative Publishing

Cooperative publishing is a publishing process independent of the traditional model where authors (and sometimes editors and designers) form a cooperative in which each member contributes both financially and in writing-editing capacities to publish works by the members of the cooperative. This approach is very old or very new, depending on your point of view. We'll explore it further later in the book. In the meantime, it's important to note that in terms of financial compensation, the members of a true co-op all take the same percentage of the royalties from any of the publications.

E-Publishing

E-publishing is digital electronic publishing where both the process and the product are digital. Traditional publishers, independent traditional publishers, self-publishers, etc., can all utilize e-publishing for production and distribution. When e-publishing first began, it was often a route that was taken after a book was published in hard copy. Today, many books, as well as journals and magazines, are available *only* electronically.

Hybrid Author

I think that it's safe to say that there is much confusion between the terms hybrid publishing and hybrid author. Unless we can make a clear differentiation, we can't communicate about it, as I mentioned at the outset of this glossary. So, I'm going to go with a clear distinction between the two. A hybrid author is one who has published books and/or other pieces through both the traditional publishing model and self-publishing.

Hybrid Publisher

Hybrid publishing is a concept that has been defined in various ways. It has also been used synonymously with the terms "author-assisted publishing" and "co-publishing." A hybrid publisher is one that encompasses aspects of both traditional and self-publishing, taking a kind of middle ground. Such a publisher may have a traditional model of acquiring your book, but they will ask you to pay for services such as editing and manuscript set-up once the book is accepted for publication. It is essentially a specific kind of business model. How they pay you varies, but it is likely to be based on a royalty model.

Imprint

In the publishing world, the term imprint identifies the name of a book's publisher. However, it's important to note that any publishing company could have several imprints that they use as divisions under the overall umbrella. For example, Simon and

Schuster, one of the so-called big-six publishers, has many imprints, including (but not limited to) Pocket, Free Press, Scribner, Athenaeum and Touchstone/Fireside. It's also important to note that when you self-publish a book, you might produce it under your own imprint (either your own name or a business name you select) or that of the supporting self-publishing platform. This is important when it comes to the application for an ISBN number which, as part of its code, identifies the publisher.

Independent Publisher

The definition of what constitutes an "independent publisher" is a tricky one because there is a difference between being an independent publisher and the act of publishing independently (see below as in, indie author). For my purposes, an independent publisher uses a traditional publishing model of acquiring work from an author and shouldering the burden of the financial responsibilities while at the same time maintaining independence from the big, corporate publishing houses.

True independent publishers are usually relatively small operations whose publishing decisions are made by individuals rather than publishing committees, as is the approach in the large houses. They will be interested in the marketability of a book, but it doesn't seem to be as large a part of the decision process as it seems to be in the large publishing houses. (I'm sure that some publishers would completely disagree with this, but it's a perception based on my own experiences.) Independent publishers pride themselves in not being a part of the so-called "big six."

Indie Author

"Indie author" is a widely used term among "indie authors" themselves and, for my purposes, refers to anyone who chooses to publish without the benefit of a traditional publisher. An indie author may go it completely alone or may hire other services such as editing and cover design services. In this case, the indie author does the sub-contracting alone. It is neither a positive term nor is it a negative term—it is simply a term. It does not refer to an author who publishes through an independent publisher as I have defined it.

ISBN Number

ISBN stands for International Standard Book Number. The number is a code that identifies the book's country, region or language, the publisher or its imprint, and its format (e.g., paperback, hardcover, electronic). Each number is unique and provides a specific identity for your book. For example, booksellers need them to identify and select your book to offer to their customers. Indeed, without such a number, your book will not be able to be as widely distributed. However, if your book is simply for your personal friends and family, and you don't expect to actually ever sell any, you don't need an ISBN. The ISBN is acquired by the publisher—if you are the publisher, then you'll need to obtain one (although some of the self-publishing platforms will do this for you).

It's also important to know that each country has different providers. For example, if you are in Canada, you will register with Collections Canada, a government agency, online, and you can obtain free ISBN's. In the USA, you can register with Bowker who will charge you a fee for the number. Finally, keep this in mind: if a publisher obtains an ISBN for you, then the code in the

ISBN will identify them as the publisher of record. This is true both for traditional publishing and self-publishing companies.

Literary Agent

A literary agent is in the business of finding publishers for authors and negotiating their contracts. They work on a percentage basis, and a reputable agent will never charge you a fee. If you query an agent who gets back to you by telling you there will be a "reading fee," run as fast as you can. Unknown writers often ask if literary agents are necessary. The truth is that you can certainly be published by a traditional publisher without an agent, but not likely by a large, mainstream publisher. If you look closely at their submission requirements, you will often see a little note that says, "No unagented work considered," or something to that effect. Don't bother sending them your work directly if they indicate this; you will be wasting your time. If you're set on a specific publisher with this policy, you'll have to find an agent first. Recently, there has been buzz about literary agents for self-published authors. At this stage, as a writer poised to self-publish, there is really no reason to have an agent, but given the changes to the publishing industry as a whole, there is little doubt that in the future, agents will redefine their role, and they will offer services to indie authors.

Literary Publisher

This is a term that I struggle with. Self-proclaimed literary publishers will be able to tell you, nose in the air, precisely what they do. However, looking in from the outside, it is not quite so clear. So, for my purposes, I am defining a literary publisher as a traditional publisher, usually of the independent variety (see below), who refuses to wear the title of trade publisher, believing that their works are a cut above in artistic or literary merit. Lately, I have seen the term "commercial literary fiction" used by agents. I wonder if this isn't an attempt to suggest that some literary work can be commercial, a characteristic that would elicit horror from traditional literary publishers. However, it depends entirely on how you define what is literary. Some definitions of so-called literary books suggest that the work simply embodies a level of complexity that defies genres.

Manuscripts: Unsolicited/Solicited

An unsolicited manuscript is one that you, the author, send to a publisher or agent without an invitation to do so. On the other hand, solicited manuscripts are those that have been invited to be submitted. So, how might you receive such an invitation? You usually begin by sending a query letter to a traditional publisher (or a literary agent), pitching both your book and you as a writer. If the publisher is interested, an editor will ask to see more. The next submission you make to that publisher will be under the rubric of the "solicited" variety. When you research traditional publishers, you'll often note that they say they do not accept unsolicited manuscripts. They really mean it.

Predatory Publishing

The concept of predatory publishing is linked to the new open-access publishing in the academic world. If you are a scholar with a book or journal to publish, you should read this. If not, you might skip down to the next definition. To understand predatory publishing, you first need to understand open access.

The new digital publishing platforms online have made it possible for the academic community to publish their work and make it widely available to other scholars and those of us in the general public. A credible open-access journal, for example, uses a peer-review process identical to that used in the more traditional journals to select papers for publication. Occasionally, even credible journals also charge the writer(s) an administrative fee that would be payable only after acceptance of the material in these cases. This is where the predatory publishers come in.

They are a new breed of open-access publishers designed to lure unsuspecting academics who need to publish to keep their jobs. According to Jeffrey Beall, writing in *Nature* in 2012, predatory publishers:

> *"...publish counterfeit journals to exploit the open-access model in which the author pays... [they] are dishonest and lack transparency. They aim to dupe researchers, especially those inexperienced in scholarly communication. They set up websites that closely resemble those of legitimate online publishers and publish journals of questionable and downright low quality."*

He further suggests that although most indicate that they are located in the US, Canada, the UK, or Australia, they are most often in places like Pakistan and Nigeria, where there is often less oversight.

It could be said that many self-publishing platforms for authors, other than academic authors, could be equally accurately described as predatory.

Publishing Independently (see also Self-Publishing)

When authors decide to forego the submission-rejection-submission-rejection merry-go-round of the traditional publishing world, they step into the world of publishing independently. The author takes full financial responsibility and can choose from various types and sizes of self-publishing and supported self-publishing platforms. The possibilities are almost endless: from companies who will simply print your book on-demand or distribute it electronically offering—but only if you want them—other services to giant behemoths like iUniverse who sell a wide variety of expensive packages and individual services and will continue to market to you even after you've said no if you publish with them. (I know this from sad personal experience and an extraordinary amount of anecdotal evidence from other self-published authors.)

Trade Publisher

A trade publisher is, in contrast to a scholarly press, for example, a traditional publisher that produces books for what is referred to as a *trade audience*. A trade audience is you and me in our everyday lives. This is a very general term. A trade publisher might specialize in fiction of a certain type, or nonfiction – but only nonfiction that has a wide appeal. If you are an academic with a thesis or dissertation you'd like to see published, step away from the trade publishers unless your plan is to significantly revise your work to make it appealing to a general readership.

Traditional Publisher

A traditional book publisher is an organization—very large, very small or somewhere in between—that takes the financial responsibility for all aspects of publication, including acquisition, editing, publishing, distributing and promoting. Consequently, this publisher garners a hugely larger percentage of the book receipts than does the author of said piece, and it must be noted maintains, by contract, complete control over many aspects of the process, from the final cover chosen to pricing, for all books they publish. Traditional publishers often make their publishing decisions from an array of solicited and unsolicited manuscripts largely based on their predictions about marketability. Judging from the number of traditionally acquired flops and notable manuscripts that they passed on, they are not very good at making these decisions. (You probably know that J. K. Rowling's original Harry Potter manuscript was rejected at least a dozen times.)

The term "legacy publisher" is increasingly used to mean the same thing as "traditional publisher."

Self-Publishing

Self-publishing differentiates itself from vanity publishing in that the term vanity has been dropped. That's really all there is to it. Make no mistake about it: self-publishing is vanity publishing without the moniker. The twenty-first century has provided self-publishers with a digital world wherein the possibilities are almost endless. Self-published books can be as bad as most publishing snobs always thought vanity-published books were, or, equally, may very well be as good as any book out there.

Self- publishing is differentiated from traditional publishing in that the author takes *complete financial responsibility* for the editing, publishing, distribution and marketing aspects of authorship and reaps the lion's share of the benefits. It need not have the stench of "vanity" about it. But it might. Note: Self-publishing need not be done under the imprint of another entity such as a publisher. However, sometimes, a large self-publishing company will require that they be the publisher of record under certain circumstances. (Refer back to the definition of ISBN.)

Subsidy Publishing

Subsidy publishing is characterized by a financial subsidy that is provided to an author by a third party to partially cover the costs of publishing. The subsequent publishing is usually done through a traditional publisher. Some people suggest that subsidy publishing is the same as vanity or self-publishing. However, that ignores the situations where subsidies are offered by non-profit or governmental organizations to support the publication of the work of academics in a scholarly publishing world where there is no money to be made, but costs need to be covered. Thus, I think it needs its own category.

Supported Self-Publishing

Supported self-publishing is a business model where a publisher provides services to a self-publishing author at a cost. They offer packages and individual services that can be purchased *à la carte,* depending on the company's size. There are large, corporate ones that try to sell various expensive services. Their business models are based on the concept of making money from selling services to authors rather than from selling books. In fact, this business model does not actually even require them to sell books at all—their profit streams accrue from selling unsuspecting authors services that, after the editing has been paid for, they often don't need. For example, they might charge you $4000 to prepare a movie treatment or up to $20,000 to turn your book into a screenplay that has no more than a minuscule chance of ever getting in front of the right people who might, just by chance, option it, and that they just on the off chance might develop it etc. A whole cottage industry of services to self-publishing authors has sprung up—for better or for worse.

Vanity Publishing

Vanity publishing is when an author pays an organization a considerable sum of money up front for the following services: editing (sometimes), formatting (usually), cover design (if you're lucky), printing and binding (always), distribution (only if you count filling the author's personal orders) and marketing (not on your life). Of course, it is self-publishing in the sense that the author pays for the company to publish a book rather than the publisher paying the author to publish that book. The term may have been used as early as the 1940s, but self-proclaimed vanity publishing expert Jonathan Clifford seems to think he coined it in 1959. The term is never used in a positive way, just as the word itself would suggest. Later in the book, I'll tell you the story of my own early foray into the underbelly of publishing that is vanity presses. Let's just say for now that the term is often used when making snide remarks about the inferiority of self-published work. Note: Vanity publishers always publish(ed) works under their own imprint.

Now that you're familiar with many of the terms used in today's publishing world, we'll explore what the confusing world of publishing looks like today.

THIRTEEN

Publishing Trends: Finding the Right Fit for You

"Writing is the only profession where no one considers you ridiculous if you earn no money."
~ Jules Renard

AS WE EXPLORED IN THE PREVIOUS CHAPTER, the publishing world of the twenty-first century is a confusing labyrinth of routes and processes that can be exceedingly difficult for new and nearly new writers to navigate. Twenty-five years ago, you would never have heard a newbie writer asking the kinds of questions that they post on online writing discussions today (for example, questions like how to find a publisher or agent or how to write a query). And you would never have seen the kinds of responses that fill those discussions because writers did their own research, and the route was straightforward.

For fiction, you wrote the book, shopped it to agents (if you were interested in big publishers), or shopped it to publishers yourself after buying a copy of the most recent edition of the reference book called *Writers' Market* (still published today) and researching smaller publishers to find out if they actually published what you wrote. You never sent a query to a publisher you knew did not publish in your genre. Then you waited.

For nonfiction, you shopped a completed book proposal to agents and publishers in the same way. And you waited. These days it's a bit like the Wild, Wild West—a free-for-all that can be exciting and exhilarating or confusing and frustrating.

I've concluded that the single most important defining feature of each of the publishing models that I've tried personally or that I've explored, comes down to one central question: *Who is paying?* (refer back to the definitions in the last chapter). And the single most important task of the unknown writer who wants to be published is to find the right publishing "fit" for a specific project, always keeping in mind that what fits for one project won't necessarily fit for the next one.

For writers trying to understand publishing trends today, the real story lies in following the money, which we'll do in this chapter.

Following the money

Way back when vanity publishing was that icky underbelly of the publishing world (at least that's how mainstream publishers and many I-wouldn't-stoop-that-low self-described literary writers thought), the main defining feature of this publishing category, if you will, was the question of who pays. And of course, as we all know, in vanity publishing, the author pays. So, if it is vain for a writer to pay for his or her work to be published, and self-publishing smacks of the same defining feature, they are one and the same—we've just sanitized our vocabulary for the sake of appearances. And the truth is if you begin to protest that there *is* a difference: availability of editing blah blah blah, you're really missing the point.

Good ideas, followed by good writing, followed by good editing, followed by good marketing is the formula for a great piece of writing and getting it into the hands of readers who might appreciate it/learn from it/ be entertained by it. There is no reason at all why this formula can't work—and work well—regardless of who is paying. Historically it has simply smacked of publishing snobbery to decry the merits of the vanity (read: self) published.

The problem, of course, remains that many indescribably bad books are published by mainstream/ traditional publishing models where the manuscript is acquired by a publisher who pays for the publishing (there is no guarantee that the publisher knows a good book from a bad one, nor is there any guarantee that the editing will be done well, but at least it will benefit from some editing); just as many unspeakably ghastly volumes are published by authors who are paying out of their own pockets. With its consequent ease of publication, the digital age has contributed to the sheer volume of bad books regardless of who is paying.

Self, vanity, traditional—these are only a few of the many models. As an example of yet another financial model, a few years ago, the *National Post's* Mark Medley published an article titled: "Words from their sponsors: Can authors cash in on crowd-sourced funding sites?" He explores the vast world of online crowdsourcing for funds for a variety of projects zeroing in on writing. I had been peripherally aware of the phenomenon of writers seeking crowd-sourced funds. Evidently, even the saintly and storied Margaret Atwood has used crowd-sourced funds. I have never really taken the time, though, to look closely. If you are the funder, there may just be a lot of money to be made on the backs of people with hair-brained ideas who can persuade others to give them seed money.

In general, here's how it works: you, the writer, sign up for one of these funders online (you know them—there are lots of them these days, and you've probably received more than one request to support some project or another far removed from writing), describe your project in a way that entices others to believe that it's a project that should see the light of day, then wait for the money to flow in. You then use the money to make it happen. You can hire an editor (if you want), hire a book designer (if you want), hire a book publicist (if you want), if you have enough money. I suppose you could also offer the money to a traditional publisher to defray the cost of publication. Still, of course, since that would be like marrying traditional publishers with the author-pays, vanity approach (there's a word in academic publishing for that: co-publishing), you'll probably get a nasty, I'd-never-touch-that-project kind of response. Unless, of course, the project is fantastic, and the publisher can see past the end of their metaphorical nose. But there are other approaches to the crowd-sourced funding publishing model that may be equally as fascinating and might have a future.

UK-based *Unbound* is a crowd-sourced publisher. They really are a publisher, but their publishing decisions and subsequent financial support to publish individual projects come not from publishing committees or their own funds, rather from "the crowd." Authors pitch their projects online and the public decides which projects are worthy of publication then pledges money to support those projects so that they see the light of day. When they hit the target number of supporters needed to move ahead with a project, *Unbound* is the imprint that publishes it.

When a selected project is funded, the writer then completes it and *Unbound* designs, edits and prints the book. The funders get copies and even sometimes get to have lunch with the author. The author doesn't pay. So, it's apparently not vanity publishing, and yet it's not self-publishing. It's a new model, and as of this writing, *Unbound* has published some 474 projects supported by over 200,000 people from 201 countries. Whatever it is, it's an innovative idea that adds to the richness of the publishing approaches. But does it make for better books? Only time will tell.

In the end, I doubt very much that it is the publishing model that has much to do with the success of a book project. It has more to do with a book that resonates with its readers who have been able to find it. Just look at *50 Shades of Grey* and its story. When it comes to commercial success in book publishing, sometimes the writing is fantastic, and other times it's epically flawed, but readers still like it.

In the end, it's really the writer who is at the heart of it in any case regardless of who pays.

Finding the right publisher: The traditional, publisher-pays route

Most of my own books have been published by traditional publishers, relying on that old and often annoying query-submission-rejection-submission-rejection-until-you-find-the-right-fit process. I have, however, also dabbled in that dark side of the publishing world – vanity publishing – and in recent years, self-publishing ventures. I think that deep-down, most writers today would really like to be published traditionally if they could, despite the moaning that goes on about losing control. There is really something satisfying about receiving that letter or email from a publisher that says, "I'm delighted to let you know that we would like to publish your book..." If nothing more, it's a bit of an endorsement for all that hard work. At least one person (or the publishing committee) liked it.

All that being said, finding the right fit for your work requires effort, as I've learned through the years. And make no mistake, finding the right fit for going it alone also takes work to get it right. Let's first explore the processes in finding the right fit if you've decided you'd like to try to get on that merry-go-round of the traditional/legacy publisher route for your book. Then we'll explore the issues to finding the right self-publishing model.

The bottom line when seeking traditional publication is that if you fail to find that right fit in the first instance, the publishers to whom you send your work will simply send you a rejection letter or email (or they'll simply ignore you), and that's so hard on the ego. I've been published by a variety of publishers—types, sizes and countries (USA, Canada, UK)—and along the way, I've learned a few things about finding that crucial right fit. The first two steps I recommend are as follows:

Find a publisher that actually publishes in the genre that you want to sell to them. This seems like a no-brainer to me. The very first time I wanted to sell a book to a publisher, I knew that it would be pointless to send it to a publisher with no interest in books about health-related topics. Publishers usually state very clearly on their web site (on the prospective author/ submissions page) about what they do and do not publish. This first step is also applicable to the search for an agent.

Find a publisher whose books are targeted toward the same readers that yours is. And forget about writing to the publisher's needs rather than the audience you intend for the book. When I first started writing, I was clearly focused on health-themed trade books. I had an idealized notion that I would "educate" the public about health issues, so I had to find a publisher whose books reflected that. I had to examine their current and back-list to see what they'd done before because publishers are not likely to see your book as the one that pushes them toward a different audience. If they only publish children's books, then forget about sending them your romance novel!

Once you've narrowed your search and have a list of publishers whose catalogue reflects the type and readership of your own material, you still have a few more steps before you can submit your work.

- *Research their submission requirements.* This is important. I cannot stress the magnitude of this enough. If you don't follow their requirements to the letter, they are not going to read your submission. Your submission is the packaging of your ideas and your package needs to conform to their specific guidelines. **If you're submitting nonfiction**, you'll need to determine exactly what they're looking for in terms of a book proposa—the format, content and length. Not all publishers want the same things, but all of them cover some important bases: Can you succinctly state the purpose and market for your book? What is it about? Why are you the right one to write it? How is it structured? What's in each chapter? When will it be finished? How long will it be? (Review the section on book proposals in Chapter Two.) **If you're submitting fiction**, do they accept unagented books? How much of the novel do they want to see? If you send too much, they might not read it.
- *Make sure that your query conforms exactly to their requirements.* This is a non-negotiable issue for unpublished writers. And frankly, why would you not follow their guidelines in preparing your submission? It shows that you are professional, you are smart, and you are interested enough in them as your potential publisher that you took the time to educate yourself about them.
- *Submit the query in precisely the method they prefer.* Do they accept email submissions? If so, should it be an attachment or a query in the body of the email? Or must you fill out an online

form? Must you send a hard copy? How many copies do they need? Do they want a self-addressed, stamped envelope for a response and/or return of the materials? When I first started writing and sending materials out to publishers, this latter approach was the only way they could be submitted. That meant making photocopies and sending large envelopes with folded envelopes inside and waiting months for a response in the mail. The truth is you might still wait months even with an emailed submission.

- *Send your query to the right person if possible.* Do a little research and find out which of the editors actually acquires (and therefore presumably enjoys) the kind of material you are sending. Then you can address your query to the right individual which is far preferable to sending it to the info@email address on the web site.

Since the very earliest days of my own writing career, it has seemed only logical that a writer ought to find out who is the most interested in a particular project then focus there. The more specific you can be in directing your query, the less time you will waste and the greater the possibility of success.

Finding the right publisher: The self-publishing-author-pays route

If you aren't prepared to get on that merry-go-round to the traditional publishing contract for whatever reason, or it is simply unimportant to you that your book at least makes the round of the traditional publishing world, then you might consider self-publishing—but from the very beginning, remember that it will cost you money to do it right. How much money it costs depends on which approach you choose. Finding the right self-publishing fit is a bit different from finding the right traditional publisher. Here are some decisions you'll have to make as you move toward deciding on an approach. You are more in control when you are in this situation, but you still need to be honest with yourself about what you're willing to do for what outcomes.

Determine how much money you are willing and able to spend. A corollary of this decision is considering the answer to the following question: *Who do you want to read your book?* The more widely you expect to distribute your book, and the more people you expect will read it will cost you more money to produce a quality product. For example, you will certainly have to pay for editing services if you expect people to take you seriously.

Decide how much work you are willing to do alone. If you want to go it completely alone (writing, editing, proofing, formatting, designing your cover, marketing: exhausted yet?), you can simply go to a print-on-demand publisher and give copies to your family and friends. You can also select electronic publishers and make your book available that way without an ISBN and sell it yourself through your own web site for example. A willingness to get other experts involved and paying them for their services enlarges the possibilities for you and your book.

Decide if you want only an e-publication or only hard copy or both. Different kinds of online publishing services provide varying products. More about this later.

Decide where you want to distribute your book. Do you want the book on Amazon, Chapters Indigo, Barnes & Noble, or Kobo? Or all of the above? In big box bookstores? In small, independent bookstores? On your website only? From the trunk of your car?

Armed with your own personal answers to these questions and considerations, you are now ready to begin your research to find that perfect fit. Be warned, though, there are hundreds of services available to you today. There is everything from the simplest print-on-demand or electronic-only formatting to behemoths of the industry that will happily provide you with every imaginable service, some of which you need, many of which you do not—for a price. Do your research carefully and keep meticulous notes about each one you are considering so that you can find one that fits your own requirements.

Now that you've considered which route you will take, it's time to dispel some of the myths about traditional publishing and self-publishing. It's time for a dose of reality.

FOURTEEN

The Publishing Process: Realities of Traditional Publishing

"Digitization is certainly challenging the old ways of doing things, whether that's in publishing or politics. But it's not the end. In many ways, it is just the beginning."
~ Heather Brooke (American journalist)

BACK IN THE OLD DAYS when I first started writing books, the only credible way to consider yourself an "author" was to find a publisher who would take on the burden of getting your book from its position in a file folder on your desk into the hands of a reader. At the beginning of this book, I told you that I'd learned early on that I'd have to sell a book three times: first to an editor, second to a bookstore and third to a reader. Further along the way, this morphed into five times: agent, editor, marketing committee, bookstore, reader. The digital age has made much of this seemingly more streamlined, but essentially nothing has changed:

the traditional model still requires writers to give up much control and most of the money in exchange for the often-considerable resources in editing and distribution and overall burden of publishing that comes especially with large publishers. The self-publishing model (and its many variations) permits the author to keep complete control: but at a significant cost. The cost might be actual money, out-of-pocket to pay for editing services, ISBN registration, design services, marketing etc.—or other costs such as a lack of quality and no sales—and not to forget the psychological burden of going it alone. Whichever route you choose, there is a price to be paid. We'll begin here with a focus on traditional publishing and follow up in the next chapter with a discussion of self-publishing models.

My own experience in the submission-rejection-submission process—with both publishers and agents—provides the framework for this discussion of what happens in the traditional publishing route examining the good the bad and the truly hideous.

Near the beginning of this book, I told you the story of my first foray into book publishing. It was the late 1980s and the only choices you had as an aspiring author were to vanity publish (we'll talk more about my adventures in vanity publishing in the next chapter), or to get on the merry-go-round that is traditional publishing. I started my journey by getting on that merry-go-round.

So, you have a book manuscript: Now what?

How do I find a publisher? That is the number one question posed on writers' forums around the world, all over the Web. The traditional approach to becoming a published author was, and remains, the following:

- Thoroughly research publishers who publish your type of book as I have already discussed (narrative or prescriptive nonfiction, literary fiction, genre fiction, children's books etc.).
- Determine if the publishers will accept unagented manuscripts.
- If yes, prepare a query based on their specific instructions.
- If no, begin a search for an agent (see below).
- Await response.
- Begin the process again (and again) if they reject you. (For a bit of solace in the rejection process, you might consider reading *The Most-Rejected Books of All Time (Of the Ones That Were Eventually Published)* at https://lithub.com/the-most-rejected-books-of-all-time/ . You'll be delighted to see the list of bestsellers that were rejected numerous times by publishers).

How do publishers make their decisions?

Perhaps more than any other mystery for the would-be author is the inscrutability of the decision-making process within traditional publishing houses. For any single one of us who has been rejected (often numerous times) there is little understanding of how the decision not to publish was made. A surf through any online bookstore will provide the opposite question: How did they decide to publish some of the schlock that comes out of traditional publishing houses alongside the works of genius or plain good writing? Even though I've been published numerous times by these traditional houses, I'm still a bit in the dark about the process, but we'll try to shed some light on it together.

One thing I do know for sure: the content of the book itself, and its quality, are not the only factors used in the acquisitions process in publishing houses. The *acquisitions editor*— the one whose job it is to find and pitch new projects to the rest of the gang in-house—is bombarded unmercifully by all kinds of full and half-baked ideas from would-be authors. It is then his or her job to sift through these ideas that come from every direction to find projects that are in line with the company's mission and interests and projects that the editor can personally get behind. The acquisitions editor must love the work. Once those issues are out of the way, the publishing house has to make a profit, so marketability of the book is a key component of the process. Depending on the size and mission of the publisher, this plays more or less into the process.

Writing in *HuffPost* in 2017, Susan Kietzman offered the following:

"Publishers don't decide which books they're going to publish while sitting alone in a dark room with one little lamp burning... Rather, this initial step in the traditional publishing process — where a book is chosen for print and its author receives an advance — is collaborative and driven by business decisions..."

Traditional publishing houses often have weekly meetings of what they call their *Editorial Board* where editors pitch projects they'd like to see the company publish. Other members of this board include marketing, sales and publicity alongside sales directors and editors. As you can see, this is a business meeting, not a meeting of literary minds.

Advance preparation for these meetings involves each acquisitions editor reading all or part of the submissions which are then read by editorial assistants and sometimes even outside readers before they ever make it to the table. Once on the table, the projects can be accepted, declined or deferred for further research or information gathering. These days, some of the data editors need to include in their pitches relates to prospective sales which incorporates an analysis of potential profits and losses.

But back to the comment above about the notion that publishers not making decisions sitting alone in a room: one of my books—a memoir—was published by a very small Canadian publisher where all of the acquisitions decisions were, in fact, made by the owner herself with input from a few trusted readers. Despite the influence of editorial boards, it has to be noted that not all publishers are the same. And size does make a difference.

Even if you do your research well, write a terrific (at least in your mind) book, the decision made by the publisher, whatever their process, might not be one you like.

So, you've been rejected: Now what?

We've all been there: we've all been rejected for something. Perhaps you didn't get into your first-choice college or university. Perhaps you tried out for a play and didn't get the part. Maybe you applied for a job and didn't get it—even after a fantastic interview. My son happens to have trained as a ballet dancer and had a successful career in that field before moving to the West End of London, back to musical theatre. But before he landed his dream job in Europe, he auditioned unsuccessfully for several companies, and I remember him telling me that in ballet school it was an underlying theme that their whole lives would be one audition after another. Isn't that really what life is all about? And as a writer seeking publication, you may well have to audition over and over and over again.

In the same way, my own work has been rejected numerous times by agents, publishers, and I suppose by readers who decided not to buy the books for whatever reason. But I've also had successes, as you have and as you will. What do these rejections look like? And how do you cope?

Even Isaac Asimov is quoted as having said: *"Rejection slips, or form letters, however tactfully phrased, are lacerations of the soul, if not quite inventions of the devil—but there is no way around them."* In my view, rejections come in three packages: the total-lack-of-response rejection, the form-letter rejection, and the almost-form-letter rejection. Let's look at each one in turn.

The total-lack-of-response rejection

I think this is the most frustrating kind of rejection because you're never sure when it has kicked in. In my experience, this happens most often with agents. Publishers will usually at least send you a form letter or email. When a publisher's or agent's web site says, "If you haven't heard from us within three months, you can consider that we've passed on your project," I see red. Although it is true that publishers are swamped with queries and manuscripts from wannabe writers, it seems to me that the writers who took the time to send them a well-crafted query at least deserve a form-letter rejection. After all, if you're a publisher or a literary agent, you signed up for this.

Providing even a form rejection would allow the writer to move on. This kind of rejection is especially galling when they have also asked that you not submit to more than one publisher at the same time: the multiple submission. The time it then takes to move on is unacceptable. This is just disrespectful.

The form-letter rejection

The form-letter rejection is so ubiquitous, some writers paper their walls with them. In the old days (and still today for some dinosaurs of publishers and agents), the submission requirements would indicate that you were to provide a SASE (self-addressed, stamped envelope) with your submission so that they could send you a photo-copied form rejection. I did not for one moment believe that if they really intended to accept your manuscript, they would object to footing the bill for a stamp, or even better, a telephone call.

These days, the form-letter rejection is really in the form of a form-email. It goes something like this:

"Thank-you for your query. While we feel that it might be a worthwhile project, we don't think it is right for us. Good luck."

What's interesting about this, is how when tweaked a bit, it can make you believe you have received a personal note of rejection when it's really a form. But don't kid yourself.

The almost-form-letter rejection

Just a tweak here and there, and you have the and the almost-form-letter rejection, which sounds like a personal note, but is what the agent or publisher always says to soften the blow. In fact, that is the purpose of this kind of rejection: to make you feel less bad about being rejected. Here are several I received from agents:

"Dear Patricia Parsons: I appreciate the intention of this work but regret I simply don't think I would be the best match. Best of luck. Sincerely…"

Or how about…

"This isn't right for me, but thanks and good luck. Best regards…"

Or…

"Dear Patricia, Thank you for the opportunity to review your project. While I appreciate that you thought of me for your work of nonfiction, I'm not sure that this project is the best fit for me. Thank you again, and best of luck in finding the right literary agent for your work. Best…"

So, the work just wasn't a good fit. I feel better now. Not really. There is nothing in any of these to suggest that the work is good, bad or indifferent. And I wouldn't expect it to say that. What you need to understand about these rejections is that *they do not reflect any kind of assessment of the value or quality of your work whatsoever.* They simply mean the agent doesn't want to represent you, or the publisher has no interest in publishing your book.

Occasionally, you do receive a much longer letter from an acquiring editor whose interest was, at least, momentarily piqued. These are much longer letters that often even suggest other publishers or agents that might be a better match or who might actually be looking for your kind of work. If you don't receive a note that is longer than three or four lines, understand **that it is what they always say—even if the work is a piece of crap and they think so.**

So, you might wonder why editors and agents do this. Sometime editor Jenn Glatzer puts it this way:

> …when…we…would like to be honest with the writer, some of us bite our tongues anyway. The reason? Not all writers know what it means to be a professional. And not all of them can take criticism. Whenever I sent constructive criticism with a rejection, I knew there was about a 75% chance I'd hear nothing back (which was fine), a 5% chance I'd get a quick "thanks for your consideration anyway" (which was nice), and a 20% chance I'd get an argument (which was not fine).

It would never occur to me to respond to an editor in any way—especially not in an argumentative tone. In the future, I might want to submit a different project to the same editor. The second reason I wouldn't do it is that it would be a waste of my precious writing time. The third reason: it is so unprofessional. Just don't do it. (Consider reading the entire blog post. The link is in the "sources" section at the back of this book.) However, if the agent or editor has taken the time to provide some constructive criticism, send that person a thank-you note.

If editors or agents are truly besotted by your work, they'll say so, and they'll ask for more. However, just because they ask for more doesn't mean that it will get published. Remember the final publishing decision is up to more than the first-contact editor.

Dealing with rejection

If you're going to be a published writer, and you want to be published by one of the big houses, or even a small independent, you have to get used to rejection. The only way to avoid rejection is to never put yourself out there and self-publish—but then you might be rejected by readers, so a discussion of dealing with rejection might be helpful even if you go that route (which we'll discuss further in the next chapter). So, how can you deal with it and even use it to add momentum to your future work?

Of course, you could simply throw up your hands and give up writing. However, in my experience with writers, this is very uncommon.

There is a streak of tenacity that seems to run through writers everywhere. There is a need to pursue it to say, "I'll show them…" So, you might begin by reviewing some books that were rejected and then went on to garner considerable success.

According to *Literary Rejections*, Dan Brown's book *The Da Vinci Code* garnered the following rejection statement: "It is so badly written." Regardless of what you might think of this book (and Dan Brown's writing), the editor who rejected it must be viewed as one who failed to spot a bestseller to the tune of some 80 million copies.

Another editor equally lacking bestseller acumen said this: "Too radical of a departure from traditional juvenile literature." The book? *The Wizard of Oz*—and we all know how that story ended: 15 million books, a perennially popular movie, cartoons, follow-ups and the list goes on.

If relishing the thought that many pieces of now-classic literature failed to fire up reams of editors and literary agents doesn't make you feel a bit better, the next approach to dealing with the rejection is to go back and regroup on two fronts. First, revisit your rejected manuscript and ask yourself how it could be improved. The second front is to go back to your research on publishers and agents to determine if, in fact, it isn't a good fit for them.

After as many rejections as you can take, you might consider putting the manuscript in a drawer (or an electronic folder) and moving on to a new project. Let what you learned by working on the first one contribute to the improvement of your ideas and your writing as you move into new territory. You might just find that the new direction eventually sends you back to the first one with a fresh eye that takes it to publishable territory.

The final frontier for the traditionally oriented author, when faced with multiple rejections, is to move into the fresh territory of self-publishing. This is not always the wisest decision—but it's where publishing is going. Stay tuned.

FIFTEEN

The Publishing Process: Realities of Self-publishing

"The good news about self-publishing is you get to do everything yourself. The bad news about self-publishing is you get to do everything yourself." ~ Lori Lesko

WAY BACK IN 2009, TIME MAGAZINE PUBLISHED an article by Lev Grossman titled "Books Gone Wild: The Digital Age Reshapes Literature." Grossman tells the now-familiar story of neuroscientist Lisa Genova's attempts to get her first novel published after pursuing all the traditional approaches: agents, queries, submissions etc. Blah, blah, blah—those of us who write books of any kind have been there. Done that. Sick of it.

You may also already know the rest of the story. She took matters into her own hands and went to the self-publishing behemoth iUniverse, published the book herself and was subsequently offered half a million dollars from Simon and

Shuster, one of the major legacy publishing companies. And you've probably all read *Still Alice* (I have not), or at the very least at this point, seen or heard about the movie. That's becoming like an urban myth. And it does speak to our continuing need to be validated by "real" (traditional) publishers as opposed to those do-it-yourself approaches. I think that most aspiring novelists would welcome this kind of outcome in any case. I'm probably among them: traditional publishers seem to want only my nonfiction. But what is so different about fiction and what lies in the future for how those stories get from a writer's head into a reader's hands?

Grossman put it this way in his article: "We think of the novel as a transcendent, timeless thing, but it was shaped by the forces of money and technology just as much as by creative genius." There is likely no doubt in your mind by this point in our explorations of the publishing world that *money and technology are perhaps the two most essential factors in the industry today*. I submit to you that they are also part of the good, the bad and the really ugly. And they are the provenance of many of the myths about book publishing.

The good, the bad and the truly hideous

Writers need money to be able to continue with their habit. Some might do it for the love of it only, but there are many others – and many of the for-love-only types as well—who would like to be paid to write. Making a living strictly on the avails of writing, however, is a whole different issue. If you want to make money from your writing and are eventually able to do so, that should count as one of the "good" parts of publishing. Publishers are clearly in business to make money: that's good for their employees but bad for writers since writers are typically the worst paid contributors to the process. Full stop. That's when the money part gets really ugly.

Technology is a really good part of publishing. It first started with the word processor back in the dark ages. I remember when I had to make final book manuscript corrections on hard copy page proofs, and any changes after that were very costly indeed. (Actually, receiving page proofs was always exciting!) Technology has changed all that. That's a good thing. Further, technology has advanced to the point where books are more accessible than ever. Of course, you might need to revisit the definition of what constitutes what we know as a "book" based on the paper versus digital divide.

Technology has also allowed all of us to be publishers. Is this a good thing? Maybe it is. However, it is also a bad thing since there are often no editors, no filters, no quality control. And that's where self-publishing gets downright hideous.

You might have the best possible piece of literature, and if a traditional publisher takes it on, it gains credibility, whether you like that idea or not. In a way, it's like third-party endorsement.

If you publish it yourself, it is suspect in some, perhaps many, circles. That's ugly since the number of poorly written, unedited, crappily-designed self-published books gives everyone a bad name. And there are some dreadful pieces of work around. We live in an age where everyone seems to think they're outstanding, even when they're not. All we need to do to verify this is to take a look at some of those so-called reality talent contests on television. You will see plenty of negative reactions from people who can't carry a tune in a bucket but are personally insulted to be told this. In contrast, others who are genuinely talented are often the most modest.

So, where does all of this leave the unknown writer who truly wants to be published? It should perhaps leave all of us closely examining the quality of our work, our motivation for publication, our publication objectives, our odds of success (if that's one of the objectives), and our commitment to going it virtually alone. Perhaps we then consider self-publishing.

What exactly is self-publishing?

Lots of places define self-publishing simply as publishing projects that authors pay for themselves. I'm going to dispute that definition to see if we can't come up with a better understanding of the varieties of models available today. My own backstory in publishing informs my personal perspective, as you will see as we move through our exploration of what precisely is meant by self-publishing. Let's begin by considering some of the definitions I've found online.

Wikipedia (arguably an authority on online self-publishing) defines self-publishing as "the publication of any book or other media by the author of the work without the involvement of an established third-party publisher. The author is responsible and in control of the entire process..." Clearly, the basis of this definition is the absence of an *established third-party publisher*, which naturally begs the question of what precisely is an *established third-party publisher*? Does this mean that if your friend says, "I'll publish your book if you pay and you can have complete control," this qualifies? Third-party, perhaps, but established? So, then what does it mean to be "established"? Does that mean if you or I open a new publishing house, we are a party to self-publishing because we haven't been around long? Or are we all right if we're incorporated? So many questions, so much vagueness.

Writing in *Publishing Perspectives*, Edward Nawotka moans about self-publishing being too, well, selfish. He suggests that so-called self-publishers can only call themselves a "publisher" if they have worked to publish someone else's work at some point in their careers. He says the following:

> *"It's my personal belief that a DIYer or self-publisher should not call themselves a "publisher" until they take risk and responsibility for publishing another person's work, which in turn is taking responsibility for another author's wellbeing. Yes, you can argue the semantics of it as much as you like, but until that point, a self-publisher is merely a "printer" (digital or conventional, sophisticated or not) adopting an honorific that they don't deserve."*

From my perspective, I think he's nailed it in one important respect. Unless you, as an author, are prepared to take full responsibility for your work and act as a publisher rather than getting an online, so-called self-publishing business to do it for you, you are not really publishing—you are merely printing & distributing your work. There are excellent values within the traditional publishing business that I believe are important to keep in mind, and the quality of the editing is an important one.

Why, though, do people get so bent out of shape when this is the reality? You can print and distribute your own work, an approach for which you indeed take all the risk and responsibility. Is there something shameful in this? You can hire (and make no mistake about it, you are hiring) a new breed publisher like iUniverse who will take over the publishing process and allow you to purchase some of the services of traditional publishers for a fee.

The advent of print-on-demand and online retailing has changed the entire landscape of both traditional (whatever that is) publishing and the new approaches (whatever we come to define them to be).

Perhaps even more important, the online universe's participatory nature has permitted anyone with a computer and a connection to the internet to call him or herself a writer or author. All I or anyone else has to do to be "published" online is to start a blog—and it doesn't even cost anything. This is both the beauty and the curse of the online writing environment.

My first foray into real self-publishing came from an absence of print material available for an undergraduate course I was teaching at the university that provided me with my day job for many years. Over time, I had accumulated material and created first a booklet, then eventually a book. It was printed and bound by the university print shop in its original form, and I provided it to students free of charge. This was a fairly standard approach to distributing materials to students at the time. A few years later, after I had continually added new material, the book had grown substantially enough that I decided that I should print it outside the university so that it would have improved production values, and perhaps I could distribute it more widely. It was then that it occurred to me it might have an audience outside of the students in my own department at my own university.

At the time, I happened to be running an outside consultancy with a couple of employees, so my company published the book under its imprint. I did everything from layout to cover design to finding a distributor and negotiating a distribution contract. It was a good thing I had some background in graphic design by that point. I also did the promotion. Truthfully, it was one of the most satisfying projects I've ever been involved in for a couple of reasons.

I was able to see the project through from beginning to end, I had complete control, I took all the risks (financially and to my reputation), and I made all the money. I did, in fact, make back all the money I put into it and then some. It was amazing. Then, one day several years later, I decided that the book needed a new edition—another update—and I was not in the same mind-set to do the whole thing over again by myself. I had learned what I needed to learn, so I shopped it to "traditional" publishers and sold it to Lawrence Erlbaum in New Jersey (which has since become part of Routlege/Taylor and Francis), a large textbook publisher in the US. Two years ago, they approached me to write a new edition, and it continues to have a life among university and college students in corporate communications programs. And they send me a little cheque every six months.

So, does the fact that the book was eventually published through conventional channels make that book any better than it was originally? Perhaps in some people's small minds, but the first edition of the book was published exactly as I had published it myself. They bought it "camera-ready"!

I then took a foray into print-on-demand publication (arguably one of the several self-publishing models available to you) by having my first historical novel printed and distributed by *Lulu*. This online service has since grown into a more mature, supported self-publishing platform than it was at the time. It was an interesting experience, but it points to the genuine differences between the various approaches to self-publishing—models that vary from bare-bones production and distribution to the elaborate service providers that will sell you every manner of service from editing to book trailers and everything in between. Make no mistake. Their main revenue stream is based on selling services to authors rather than selling books to readers.

My second historical novel was "published" by iUniverse, one of those large companies offering vast numbers of services, whose editing and publishing services I bought (the same one that Lisa Genova turned to, as we discussed earlier). So, why didn't I sell it to a "traditional" publisher? To tell you the truth, I was exhausted by them and their lengthy processes.

Over the years, I had been published by several traditional publishers, including such trade publishers as Doubleday and academic publisher The University of Toronto Press, among others, and I'm tired of them.

I'm tired of their delays; tired of how influential their marketing departments are in the choice to publish or not publish regardless of the acquiring editor's opinion of the merits of the book; very tired of the paltry percentage of profits that are given to the person who actually wrote the book; tired of losing control of the work. I was also peeved off at a literary agent who said this to me, "If I had a dollar for every *bona fide* nonfiction author who wanted to be a novelist, I'd be rich," and then refused even to read my fiction proposal. I did not need a nonfiction agent. I had experienced considerable success at placing my own nonfiction without giving up a percentage to an agent. What I needed was an agent for fiction.

Did my experience put me entirely off traditional publishing? No, of course not. A real writer looks for the best route to publication for a specific project. Sometimes that might be wading into the traditional pool. At other times it might be jumping into the deep end of self-publishing.

It would, however, be nice to find an innovative approach that encompasses the best of both traditional and new publishing while at the same time acknowledging the writer as a more critical part of the process. I'm thinking about the notion of *cooperative publishing*, a situation in which half a dozen or so of us writers begin to work together, editing and working on one another's projects, and then publishing under a co-op imprint—something to think about.

The numbers and identities of authors in history who have self-published are astonishing. For example, were you aware that James Joyce self-published *Ulysses*? Or that Beatrix Potter published *The Adventures of Peter Rabbit* without the benefit of a traditional publisher? Then there are authors like Mark Twain, John Grisham, Walt Whitman and Edgar Allan Poe, to name a few famous, self-published authors. And there are many more.

So, perhaps it's time we recognized that self-publishing has always been a part of the literary landscape.

Is self-publishing the same as vanity publishing?

Before self-publishing had any credibility (one of my assumptions here is that it has risen a notch or two on the credibility barometer in recent years), it was referred to strictly as *vanity publishing*. Presumably, it was vain for an author to pay to have his or her book published. I've never been sure why it isn't vanity recording when a musician pays to have a CD recorded and subsequently distributed, but perhaps that is another discussion.

According to a man named Jonathon Clifford (whom I mentioned in the Chapter Eight glossary of terms), he was the individual who coined the phrase *vanity publishing* around 1960. Clifford's lifetime crusade was for honesty in the vanity publishing world. It is true that over the years, authors who could not get—or did not try to get—mainstream publishers interested in their work would pay to have their work produced, and those vanity publishers would suggest to the authors that they could, perhaps, just maybe, probably get rich. That was the problem. As Clifford says:

"If you cannot find a mainstream publisher to publish your work at their expense, you must look on the whole process of publishing not as money invested to make you a return, but as money spent on a pleasurable hobby which you have enjoyed and which has provided you with well-manufactured copies of your book. If you do also manage to make a small profit, then that should be looked upon as an unforeseen and unexpected bonus."

Today, the notion of the vanity press (versus other self-publishing options) seems to be tied into the issue of promises made by these entities—promises that they cannot possibly keep—and into their lack of editing. So, the term *self-publishing* has arisen to take the place of the much-deplored moniker vanity publishing and seems to have taken on a less pejorative connotation.

Self-publishing, from the author's point of view, though, is the same as vanity publishing. ***The author pays***. And any author who thinks a publisher, regardless of whether they make you pay or they pay you, can predict, much less guarantee, the sales success of your book, is naïve in the extreme. This is one of the most enduring myths surrounding publishing in general: that anyone has a crystal ball to predict the future success of any manuscript. Unless you have a name that is widely recognized, there is no way to predict sales. This is where my skepticism begins to creep into the relationship between author and publisher. It is now time for me to come clean, as they say.

What seems like a hundred years ago now, I did take up with one of those vanity publishers for fiction two years after a "real" publisher published my first nonfiction book.

The book was called *Confessions of Failed Yuppie*. And it was funny. It was nothing like what I had written previously. The vanity press I chose was one of the big ones in New York. They took my substantial fee and provided me with two cartons of the 130-page, hard-covered books resplendent with dust jackets. I was thrilled. But something kept me from mentioning its provenance to anyone – although I'm not sure anyone would have cared. Many of my friends read the book and told me that they were amused. So, what's wrong with this kind of model? What makes a vanity-published book or a self-published book less worthy than a book published via the more traditional publishers? In a word, quality—but not necessarily quality of the content, story, theme or writing.

It is often the quality of the editing and the production values—the cover and interior design mainly. The problem with self-publishing is that it permits you to publish without any kind of quality control. It is up to the authors to ensure that they are committed enough to the publishing process to ensure a quality product.

The process of self-publishing

There is no one right way to self-publish. It is a myth that there is a magic formula. That said, a voyage through the process might be helpful. Let's go step-by-step.

- *First, write your book.* This is self-evident, or at least it should be. However, many unknown writers begin to explore the idea of self-publishing long before they have come anywhere close to finishing writing the book. This behaviour usually indicates an infatuation with the idea of being published when the emphasis should be on the writing.

- *Second, rewrite your book.* I cannot stress this enough. A first draft is never suitable for publication. Rewrite it, put it away. Reread and rewrite it again.
- *Third, reread Chapter Thirteen.* In that chapter, I discussed finding the right fit for you when it comes to publishing. Make those decisions to help you figure out what kind of a publishing process you want to use.

Be aware that even the self-publishing process, when done right, is time-consuming and can be expensive. But for many unknown and increasingly even well-known writers, the process can be very satisfying.

Self-publishing: A cautionary tale

One day, as I approached the publication date for one of my books, I received an email from my editor at this traditional publisher. He happily reported that we were now embarking on the cover design for my new book. This was good news; it meant that we were really getting there after an exhausting journey of several years (yes, years) with this publisher with this one book.

It marked the ninth time that I had been through this traditional publishing process where control I had given over much control to the publisher. But it was at times like these that I reconsidered the traditional route in favour of self-publishing.

This reflection on my publishing adventures resulted this time from my editor's simple statement in his email: "…Time and budgetary restraints being what they are, we're unable to ask our designers to come up with a cover completely from scratch. Rather, it falls to you (and to me) …" then we would send this to the so-called designers. It seems to me that a designer should be doing the designing and if he or she isn't doing the designing, what in the world is he or she paid to actually do?

It might seem to you that this would be the moment in time when I make that decision to move to self-publishing for that next book, but I was reeling from yet another telephone call from iUniverse (the supported self-publisher I had used for a novel)—an attempt to sell me yet more services thinly disguised as a wonderful opportunity for me.

Earlier that week, during dinner time one evening (they are always at dinner time when I'm feeling just ready to punch the next telemarketer who calls despite being on the do-not-call list), the phone rang. The caller was a "marketing specialist" or consultant or manager or some such thing—iUniverse seems to either have an enormous staff or massive turnover since this was the third or fourth such person to whom I had evidently been assigned. Several incarnations ago, I had even asked them not to call me with marketing ideas ever again.

This time the approach was that my book was so good that it should be a movie. Would I be interested in having it shown to something called "Thruline Entertainment"?

I told him to send me an email and hung up (I was more polite than that, but that's the edited version of the story). The email arrived in due course (read: immediately). Here's what he said in part:

> *I called in earlier today to inform you that your book, "Grace Note" can be adapted into a motion picture. Hollywood Coverage: Your book has all the elements Hollywood wants — an exciting plot, well-developed characters and fresh content — yet there's still a crucial piece you need in order to be taken seriously by established entertainment executives.*

We would like to know if you'd be interested to have your books presented to our newly acquired partner, THRULINE Entertainment. THRULINE is a Hollywood production company and they are basically looking for good books to adapt into a movie.

The contract has just been sealed last August, and basically, we want to impress our new partner. We don't want to provide them with a "just-an-ordinary" material. We are putting our best foot forward because we want to prolong this contract.

If you're interested, your book just needs a Script coverage in order for us to present this to production companies and producers. That is the basic tool that they would look for instead of reading the whole book.

He then went on to tell me that the two-part script coverage would be done by a professional who has done this before etc. He did not tell me the price or any reference to the fact that he wanted to sell me a service, but I knew that this was precisely what was happening. And indeed, my subsequent research on Thruline uncovered a company with self-described ties to the Hollywood machine that works with self-publishing companies to part authors from their money. Well, they didn't say it that way, but I can read between the lines.

Of course, if your book really is adaptable as a movie, you can send it to an agent who does this kind of thing. Options on books can and are taken from the book itself. And doesn't it make sense that someone who is genuinely interested in adapting your book might actually have to read the book? Yes, script "coverages" are done, but really? I actually had an earlier book optioned and learned that the vast majority of optioned books never even make it to the treatment phase.

The iUniverse price for this script coverage was $859.00 (USD).

The following is what I said in my response to the email:

Thanks for this. Don't bother telephoning me. I'm not paying upwards of $900 for any more services from iUniverse. If you think the book is good enough to be sold to "Hollywood" then I think you should be willing to put up the money for a percentage on the back end. Otherwise, we have nothing to talk about. I'm an accomplished writer—I can do this myself. I think it's time iUniverse took a different tack when it comes to 'services' for writers.

But call he did. This time I didn't answer.

Self-publishing requires an author to be a writer, editor, interior book designer, cover designer, marketer and promoter (or hire these professionals as sub-contractors). So, is this so different from traditional publishing these days?

When an editor at a traditional publishing house tells me that he is "unable to ask our designers to come up with a cover completely from scratch..." it seems that the two publishing models are getting closer together.

What is the cost of publishing your book?

You might think that the question we should ask is: *How much does self-publishing cost?* But if I asked the question that way, you'd expect a number, a sum of money. Self-publishing does require wildly varying financial investments; however, there are other costs that aren't monetary—and they can be substantial. But let's deal with the money first.

According to estimates at the time of this writing, the costs for self-publication range from about $100 to about $1500, and I can tell you without a doubt that it can cost you much more.

According to the online Self-Publishing School, services that you will want/need come with the following price tags (in US dollars):

- Cover design = $100-$600
- Editing = $300-$1500
- Formatting = $50-$300
- Promotion = $0-$500
- Tools (e.g. author web site, courses, email services, writing software) = $175 and up

I can tell you that many self-published authors spent almost none of this money (and it shows) while others spent a great deal more. But this is a good place to begin.

Of course, you could go ahead and publish a piece of crap that is riddled with mistakes—or you could rely on your best friend or spouse. But if those people aren't professional copy-editors, I guarantee you that I (and all the rest of your readers) will find those mistakes that your amateurs missed. And what about your cover? These days, the cover design has been demonstrated to have an effect on whether or not a potential reader will actually purchase your book. If you want to see what can happen if your book cover isn't professional, go immediately to read "26 Hilariously Bad Book Covers" at https://www.buzzfeed.com/lukelewis/hilariously-bad-book-covers.

So, how can you decide how much to pay? Writers considering self-publishing have a vast array of choices from the no-frills, you-do-all-the-work, print-on-demand and ebook publishing platforms to the full-meal-deal supported self-publishing. But buyer beware: my own iUniverse story is that cautionary tale: they are in business to sell you many services that you probably don't want and most assuredly don't need. The gamut runs from *Lulu*, which will let you publish your book in a variety of hard copy and electronic formats for no investment at all if that's what you want. For example, they suggest that a standard trade paperback book with a glossy cover that runs 100 pages will cost about $6.00 to manufacture and distribute. You will write, do the interior design, create the book cover, write the marketing copy and format everything yourself. If you want help with any of that, you pay. That's the business model of most no-frills publishing platforms.

Then, if you invest the money, what kind of return on your investment are you likely to achieve?

The statistics on how much money self-published authors (and the majority of traditionally published authors, it has to be said) make for their efforts is truly demoralizing. Evidently, *the vast majority of self-published books sell fewer than ten copies on Amazon,* if that's any indication. In fact, *the "average" income for authors with self-published books on Amazon is less than $100 a year.* If that is "average" and there are a few successful authors in the mix (which there are), this translates into pennies—or nothing—for most of them.

The bottom line is that you have to do some research before you start the process. If you post a question on a writers' forum online asking other "writers" about the best self-publishing platform, you'll get too many disparate answers for the information to be useful. You need to go to each site yourself and read what they offer to see if it fits your objectives.

So, these are the financial costs. What other costs are there?

The psychological cost of self-publishing

You are on your own out there in the big world of publishing when you go it alone. Despite what the large self-publishing platforms say about being there for you, they are really there for themselves – they are focused on the bottom line and how much money they can make. As I have already mentioned, most of them use business models that don't rely on book sales at all. Book sales are too unpredictable. This situation means that they do not care much if you make money as long as they continue to sell their services to you, and they make money. If you were to have a bestseller, that would be a bonus, icing on the cake. But make no mistake, the only one who risks making nothing on your writing is you. Although there is no data on the subject, I suspect that this isolation is why so many online writers' groups have sprung up.

In the traditional publishing model, you always have your editor or the marketing team to complain to. The publishing company is not making any money if you don't sell books, so you and the team really are on the same page with the same objective in mind. (Although to be clear, the editor and marketers will still get their salaries until the company goes bankrupt!) If you like the idea of the freedom that self-publishing provides, and are willing to do the work needed for a great product, then you're on your way.

Indie paranormal romance author, Zoe Winters, has said, "Whatever you may have heard, self-publishing is not a short cut to anything. Except maybe insanity. Self-publishing, like every other kind of publishing, is hard work. You don't wake up one morning good at it. You have to work for that."

Reality Check #4:

Books Don't Sell Themselves: Book Promotion is Hard Work

"Publishing is a very mysterious business. It is hard to predict what kind of sale or reception a book will have, and advertising seems to do very little good." ~ Thomas Wolfe

SIXTEEN

Book Promotion 101: Who Will Read Your Book?

"Everyone is not your customer." ~ Seth Godin

BOOKS DON'T SELL THEMSELVES. This realization was probably the first reality of publishing that I learned. This was swiftly followed by its corollary: *Someone has to sell them—and that someone is mostly the author.* This is a consideration that writers who wish to see their books read by adoring fans seem to have forgotten. It is a myth that readers will magically find your book because it is in a genre that they regularly read.

Potential readers will never have the joy of reading the books that they have never heard about. We need to explore what book promotion really means in the industry overall and for individual authors. For me, my own experiences also drive home the fact that it doesn't matter whether you are traditionally published, or you take on the job yourself: *you still have to learn how to promote your work.* And you have to know who will read it.

The presumption that I make when delving into the notion of book promotion is that you actually *would* like someone to buy and read your book—or at least read it.

I say this because as hard as it might be for some unknown writers to understand, it is not a foregone conclusion that all writers care about whether others will read their work. (Of course, you might well suggest that they should then not publish – which implies "public" work—but we'll not go there at this time). For example, an academic might publish something simply to have it on the public record, knowing full well that the subject matter is discernible to a select few and there will be few readers. Even if you aren't doing this to generate income from the actual published work, you probably do want others to read it so that you can accomplish other objectives.

For example, you might write and self-publish a book because you want to share something with the hope of helping others, and you don't care if you make any money—it's a labour of love. Another reason for writing a book might be to promote your career and build your reputation as an expert in your field. Books written for this reason are what career self-help gurus sometimes refer to as your *electronic business card*. You write a short ebook showcasing your expertise. People then download it for free, read it, like it and subsequently hire you to do whatever it is you do.

The bottom line is this: ***whether for love or money, if you want someone other than you and your immediate family to read this book, you have to promote it.*** People will not buy, download, read, think about or talk about your book if they do not know it exists. It's as simple as that. The problem is that many writers don't see themselves as marketers—and for a good reason. They're just not good at it. It's time to hone your skills. And that starts with a plan.

The book promotion plan

There are two approaches—strategies if you will—to promoting your book: seat-of-the-pants-and-devil-may-care or make-a-plan-and-implement-it. That's it.

With a quarter of a century in the corporate communication strategy game, I'm not interested in the seat-of-the-pants etc., approach to book promotion or any other kind of marketing activity. If you want others to read your book, you'll have to find out who they are and figure out how to make them take action by buying and reading your book.

There's a theory about how people adopt new products and ideas. It's called the *diffusion-of-innovation theory*. In a nutshell, it suggests the following as a general, non-linear explanation of how we move to buy that book:

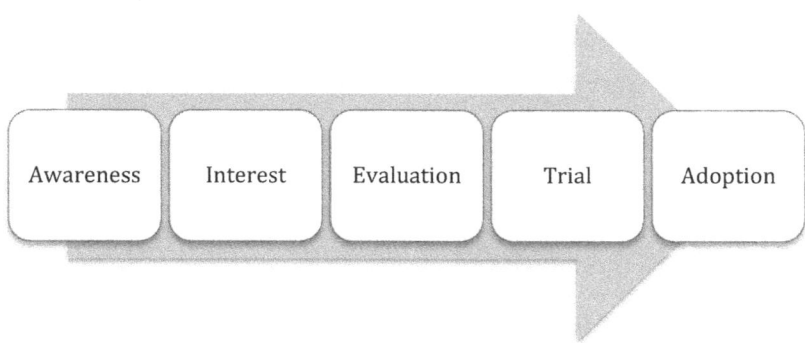

What this means is that people first have to become aware that the book exists. Then something has to pique their interest. The potential readers will then somehow evaluate—usually in their own heads—the idea that they should read the book. They may do this by reading reviews or looking for recommendations from friends and networked acquaintances or just thinking about it. They then try it out either by examining the inside of the book online, downloading a sample, or even buying a copy. The notion of *adoption* means that a reader who adopts this product (book) would tell others about it then await, with bated breath, your next book. Getting readers to do this is the holy grail of book promotion. *A single, one-time purchase by someone who hates the book is not what you're aiming for.*

If we use this understanding of the general process that potential readers would go through, we can develop a framework to guide our book marketing. That framework will have several planks that include the following:

- Identifying and locating potential readers;
- Deciding what you want to accomplish with them;
- Developing the right messages for these potential readers;
- Targeting these potential readers by using media they embrace;
- Disseminating the messages to the reader; and finally
- Measuring your success based on the objectives you wanted to achieve.

We'll examine each component in turn.

Identifying and locating potential readers

What do you know about the people who might be interested in your book? Let's begin by examining the potential readers for a work of nonfiction.

If you did what I suggested in an earlier chapter and created that book proposal for a publisher or yourself, you would have had to think about this before you even wrote the book. If for one second, you believe that your book is for everyone, you need to know right now that you're wrong. **No book is for everyone**. That means that you'll have to think carefully about what might be considered your book's *mission*.

- What is your book intended to accomplish?
- How will it accomplish its goal?
- Who is the goal intended to target?

Once you can state these things, you have your book's mission statement, so to speak. Then you can begin to figure out more details about the potential readership of your book.

Your work of fiction can be dealt with similarly, although creating a mission statement for a piece of fiction is probably a bit more esoteric. You might not have a particular goal for the book other than entertaining readers with a good story—but I believe that this is a worthy one in itself. How it will do that is through great story-telling. Who will read it and where you can find those potential readers will require just as much research as it does in finding readers for nonfiction books.

Regardless of whether you are writing narrative or prescriptive nonfiction, genre fiction, literary fiction or even poetry, here are a few questions that you need to answer before you can move into the rest of the book promotion plan.

- Is this book for men or women or both?
- Is there a particular age group to which most potential readers are likely to belong?
- Will people with certain habits or interests be more likely to buy it?
- Where do these people "hang-out"? Social media groups? In-person groups?
- Is it likely that your potential readers live in a specific country? State or province? City?
- Are they more likely to be urban or rural?
- What are their overall social media usage habits?

- Where do they go for most of their news or entertainment recommendations?

You begin to get the sense that you're really painting a word picture of who these people are. Once you know this, it is much easier to reach out to them.

When I contemplated the promotional plan for my memoir about being a ballet mom, I had to consider all of these questions. The fact that it was published through the traditional route (submission-rejection-submission-acceptance etc.) didn't change my responsibilities as an author. In the twenty-first century world of publishing, authors are responsible for the lion's share of the book promotion work, whether traditional publishers publish their books or they publish them on their own.

Your objectives and messages

Obviously, you want potential readers to buy and read your book. In fact, for many writers, accumulating readers is often the primary objective. But is this all? Do you want them to view you as an expert in your field? Do you want them to see you as a writer whose work will propel them to buy more of your books? Do you want them to engage with you on your blog? On Twitter? On Instagram? Are you using this book to establish your credentials as a springboard to career progression?

These might seem like questions you can simply take for granted. They are not. Your well-thought-out answers to them can help enormously in trying to figure out what to say to these potential readers and where to find them.

You may never have thought about this, but different messages will resonate with different readers.

What do you want to say to potential book reviewers? Do you want honest reviews (highly recommended), or do you want vanity reviews? Those are reviews that you hope to get from fellow unknown writers with a view to giving equally glowing reviews to their books. These, along with the ethically-suspect paid reviews, are not reviews at all; instead, they are advertisements.

What do you want to say to potential readers? The answer to this question will provide you with your book blurbs that will be part of your book's online description and on its cover. Your message for potential readers is a critical consideration in marketing. What you say in these blurbs and how you write them—the words you choose—will either repel or attract readers. For example, when I read an online description of a book on a site like Amazon, I expect the book to be equally poorly written if the blurb is poorly written. If it doesn't accurately portray what the book is about, I might buy it and be severely disappointed, resulting in me posting a bad review, or I might not buy it at all even though I might well enjoy it.

Sarah Juckes, writing on the *Alliance of Independent Authors* site, suggests that writing your book's blurb is the hardest part of the process because it requires you to condense "…your novel into a few, short paragraphs in a way that makes your book impossible to overlook." She then suggests some steps you can take for writing a great blurb, including doing research, finding the right style and voice, ensuring you start with a synopsis, and editing. The difference between a synopsis and a blurb is worth noting: the synopsis summarizes the entire book, whereas the blurb never provides a spoiler. Instead, it entices you to want to read more. You need that synopsis, though, before you can then distill the salient points you need for that ever-so-brief and all-important blurb.

Accuracy, clarity and style all play a part in creating a compelling message for potential readers.

Targeting your readers

Many new writers fail to consider who their specific readers are likely to be, resulting in a significant amount of wasted time and effort. Remember what we said earlier: your book is not for everyone, regardless of how much you might think it ought to be. These days, there is a tendency for new writers to spend an enormous amount of time on places like Twitter and Facebook without giving much thought to whether or not that's where their potential readers are. In the next few chapters, we'll examine these places in more depth. At this point, however, writers must understand that they might be wasting their time.

If, for example, your nonfiction book is designed for older adults, you'll need to do some research to determine their use of various media. You might find that your target readers rarely look to social media for book recommendations. On the other hand, your genre fiction might resonate well with specific groups on Facebook, Twitter or Instagram. (You need to delve into the social media habits of any target group you determine will be the ones most interested in your work. An online search of the social media habits of groups with specific demographics is simple to accomplish and will result in much useful information for you.) Or perhaps your readers usually buy their books at conventions or meetings. Knowing this is essential information for your marketing efforts.

Lifehack has published a great list of top book-recommendation sites on the web. (See the resources section for the link.) Reviewing this list would help you see where your readers go to find new books, and if you do some research on each of these sites, you'll quickly determine which sites would be useful for you and how to go about getting your book featured there.

How successful was your plan?

Figuring out the extent of your plan's success depends on what you intended to accomplish from the outset. But it is worth doing a check-in once in a while to see how effective your plan's elements are while you implement it.

If you simply consider your objective to be a numbers game, that will be your yardstick. If, however, you want to build a reputation, a brand or a loyal following, your evaluation efforts will be more nuanced and longer-term. Whatever parameters you select to measure your success, remember that you'll have to assess how you're doing from time to time to tweak your plan. As you move forward in promoting your book, you'll find that some approaches will work better than others, and you'll want to make changes along the way.

The next few chapters will provide you with a discussion of what kind of tactics you might include in your book marketing plan. Whatever you finally decide to incorporate, there is one element that I cannot stress enough: start planning early (but not while you are still writing the first draft). Book marketing planning should begin before you actually release your book. Some of the tactics we'll discuss in the next few chapters need to be executed before publication, while others simply need to be planned for implementation after that magic date.

SEVENTEEN

C's, and P's and Selling, Oh My: The Alphabet Soup of Book Marketing

"The aim of marketing is to know and understand the customer so well the product or service fits him and sells itself." ~ Peter Drucker

NO MATTER WHICH WAY YOU LOOK AT IT, unless you're writing for your vanity only, and perhaps to provide copies to your family for Christmas (I do that with cookbooks), you're going to have to find a way to market your book.

In 2014, Jennifer Alsever wrote a piece for *CNN Money* called "Guerrilla Marketing for Books." A cautionary tale for would-be authors, the article tells the story of shrinking promotional budgets at traditional publishing houses and the lengths to which authors now must go to get their books to stand out from the ever-increasing numbers of both traditionally and self-published books. The truth is, it has been ever thus. Unless you are a big-name author, you will likely need to go to some length to promote the book regardless of whether you publish it through a legacy publisher or do it yourself.

One tactic mentioned in the story describes an author who commissioned a jewelry artist to make necklaces that were featured on her book's cover and a new perfume based on one of her fictional characters. The amount of work and money involved for an author to do this is staggering to consider. Her efforts, however, reminded me of an event in the provenance of one of my own books: the early 1990s incarnation of *Confessions of a Failed Yuppie*.

In the early 1990s, I was on a rant about the Yuppie lifestyle. So, naturally, I decided to write a book about it. Rather than penning a nonfiction examination of the phenomenon, which would have been more akin to my writing experience at the time, I decided to write a novel—a satire of sorts. I felt strongly, though, that I wanted it published no matter what, so I did what self-publishing authors did at that time, I sent it to a vanity publisher

In due course, a box full of hard-cover copies of *Yuppie* arrived on my doorstep. What to do with them? Those were the days before book promotion through online networking channels was *de rigeur*. Indeed, there were no social media channels. Just imagine such a world! I decided that the first order of business would be to have a book launch, a traditional book marketing tool we'll talk about in a bit. But before the launch, I knew that I would need some "merchandise."

I created a design for the front of T-shirts and mugs and had dozens of these pieces of paraphernalia created—all at my own expense, of course—and had them available on the day of the party. I also had a poster-sized blow-up of the book's cover so that it could be the focal point of the party, next to the book-shaped cake that adorned the dining room table. I then created a guest list and sent out invitations.

As parties go, the event was a great success. We had door prizes of T-shirts that the guests obligingly sported, and everyone went home with a signed copy of the book, which I provided free of charge to them. (I've been at other such gatherings more recently where the author sold copies in a prominent place at the party.)

As the weeks went by, a number of the guests told me that they had enjoyed the book and asked when I would write another one. The book, naturally enough, never sold. Getting a self-published book reviewed in those days was not next to impossible; it was *utterly* impossible. And since there were no social networks available to promote it, short of taking out advertisements at great expense (I did that once) and going door-to-door with a pile of books (which didn't sit well with my personality), the book would languish with thousands of others. The truth is, like it or not, writers need to understand marketing and the jargon that goes along with it. As writer Seth Godin has said, *"Marketing is a contest for people's attention."*

The original 4 P's

If you've ever done any kind of studying or reading about marketing, you'll already be familiar with the term *marketing mix* and the traditional four planks that constitute it. But let's review.

The term marketing mix is nothing more than jargon for assorted tools that come together to create a marketing plan designed to sell a product or service. Perhaps more specifically, the marketing mix consists of those tools that are controllable. Understanding this is a fundamental concept if you're trying to understand how to market a book.

The original four P's are as follows:

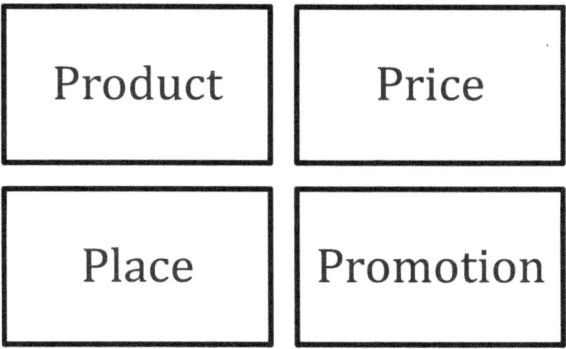

If you consider what these mean in the world of book marketing, your book is your product. Your price is how much it sells for, of course (these days we have to consider the format and the marketplace—e.g., USA, UK, Australia, Canada etc.—all of which you might have different pricing structures for; ebook versus print book). The place involves where the products will be available to potential readers (which online retailers etc.). Finally, promotion refers to the strategy and tools you'll use to ensure that potential readers will find out about your book and buy it.

Using this traditional formula, you can create a marketing plan that would look something like the following:

1. Complete (write the darn book!) and package your product (packaging would include interior format and cover);
2. Determine the price you want to sell it for in which countries;
3. Decide on where it will be available: sites like Amazon, Barnes and Noble, Chapters/Indigo to name three; your local book store perhaps; then,
4. Decide what communication tools you'll use to ensure that your potential readers know about the book. For

example, you might use Instagram, X, Facebook, TikTok, direct mail, email, or more traditional promotional tools such as author readings, book launches or advertising to promote it.

Although this framework is better than nothing, it probably isn't specific enough to the task at hand. In fact, recently, these tried and true planks have been tweaked slightly to acknowledge the realities of the twenty-first century – but perhaps not for the realities of book marketing. We'll get to that.

The new 4 C's

At the beginning of the 1990s, this traditional framework was supplemented by a newer version that consisted of what its creator, Robert Lauterborn, Professor of Advertising at the University of North Carolina and recognized advertising expert, called the *Four C's*. He suggested that to market our product, we need to consider a newer approach.

These are very similar to the original P's but put more emphasis on the consumer's needs and wants and less on the product itself. Suppose you write books because you are a writer, not a content creator who writes solely for selling. In that case, the consumer is not as crucial in developing your product as it might be in other endeavours such as creating a new cereal. In other words, you write the book that you have to write, then determine who might be interested in it (a bit counter-intuitive if you remember our discussion about knowing your readers, but that's how it is in the writer's world). In the content creation model—which is the one that most closely resembles the general product development model—you figure out what the readers want, and you write what you think they will buy. Every word and phrase you write must consider the reader. For most real writers, this is cumbersome and not why they write. It's not even why they *should* write. So, in this model of the marketing mix, the customer's wants and needs are an after-the-fact consideration.

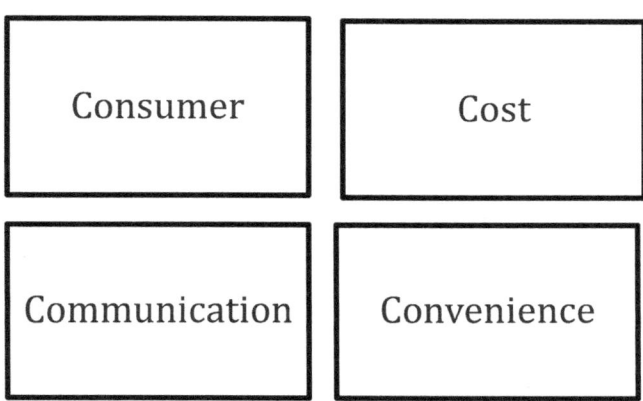

Notice that the cost is equivalent to the price in this model, but Prof. Lauterborn further suggested that the customer's actual financial cost is not the only price. In my view, these considerations are less evident in book marketing than they might be for other products. For example, if you are selling running shoes, the price you might point out to the customer is more than what you mark on the price tag. It might also be the price to be paid in leg cramps for not buying your new-fangled runners. This kind of effect is not so useful for book-buying in general, but it could be a helpful consideration in your messaging if you're selling a self-help book or the like. For example, if someone opts not to buy your book, he or she might pay the price of missing out on knowledge that would otherwise improve life. The price they pay is one of your messages.

He also proposed that communication includes not only the one-way approach suggested by the concept of promotion but also the development of dialogue with your customers, an approach that was all but impossible in my early days of book publishing in the late 1980s but is the flavour of the day in marketing in this twenty-first century. Dialogue can be a beneficial concept for authors developing their brands: creating opportunities to engage with your potential readers is a part of the new approach to promotion, primarily facilitated by social media. Keep this concept in mind as we move along.

The final C of the Four C's is convenience. Somewhat analogous to the original concept of place, this can be useful in book marketing. It requires you to figure out the most convenient place for your readers to buy this book and the most convenient way for them to pay. I remember the late American self-help author Wayne Dyer once told the story of how he achieved his first bestseller, *Your Erogenous Zones,* by taking a trunk full of books and lugging them across the country from bookstore to bookstore, essentially selling them out of his car. That would likely not be "convenient" for readers these days. But it wouldn't be a stretch for you to begin to consider where your readers would find convenient.

The alphabet of marketing a writer

At this stage, it's probably safe to say that a strictly traditional marketing approach doesn't work as well for books as it does for selling cereal—which brings us to the four planks that I think are the most helpful for you in the creation of your marketing plan for your book.

- ✓ CREATION (your book and its cover)
- ✓ COST (the price you will charge, the costs you will accrue)
- ✓ CONNECTIONS (how you are placed, your personal brand)

- ✓ *COMMUNICATION* (the tools & tactics you'll use for getting your message out)

The next few chapters will concentrate on the realities of your book's cover, the myths and the truth about traditional marketing and promotional tools you'll want to consider, and what you need to include when using the more up-to-the-minute social media approaches that will help you to develop your personal brand and ultimately help your book to find its readership.

EIGHTEEN

Your Primary Promotional Tool: Your Book Cover

"Just because you can design your own book cover, doesn't mean you SHOULD." ~ www.lousybookcovers.com

LIKE EVERYONE ELSE, YOU'VE NO DOUBT heard the phrase, "You can't judge a book by its cover." However, it is a metaphor that has nothing whatsoever to do with books and their covers. It's not really going out on a limb these days to say to writers that your book will, indeed, be judged by its cover, and this includes both its design and what's on it—your title. Further, most book promoters/marketers will suggest that it's your number one promotional tool. So, I'm devoting a whole chapter to my adventures in book covers and the lessons I've learned along the way.

First a title, then a cover

How important is a book's title? Is a book's title important to you? André Bernard, writing in a lovely little book *Now All We Need is a Title: Famous Book Titles and How They Got That Way*, tells us that John Steinbeck evidently didn't care a bit about his book titles quoting him as saying, "I don't give a damn what it's called." Bernard suggests that this was, however, "...quite untrue. Steinbeck worked hard at his titles, and the results are among the most memorable in American literature."

Unlike Ernest Hemingway, who said, "*I make a list of titles after I've finished the story or book – sometimes as many as a hundred. Then I start eliminating them, sometimes all of them,*" I am unable to write anything longer than a letter without a title firmly fixed in my mind. I absolutely must have it in front of me as I move forward as if I can somehow see the finished product, and it's beckoning me toward it. The truth is that I rarely change that title. It may require a bit of a tweak here or there, but those tweaks seldom result in much of a difference. This rule holds true for me regardless of the genre or the publication type: creative nonfiction, business books, fiction, magazine articles.

One of my book title journeys found me using a working title all through the writing process but changing it near the end. Not using at least a version of a working title is unusual for me but does indicate my flexibility!

A work of historical fiction, the novel had required several years of meticulous background research on twelfth-century Roman Catholic mysticism, the Benedictine Order and ancient music. And all through that work, the book had a title—a title I liked. It was called *The Woman in the Shadow*, and for me it represented what the book was about. Enter **the editor**.

The editor liked the story, the characterization, the theme, even the literariness of the writing (not the usual hallmark of most of my writing). The editor did not, however, like the title. At all. The editor said, "As it stands, the title doesn't tell much about the content of the book." I thought about this for a while and thought, *Maybe the editor is right.* I started thinking about book titles in general as I moved toward finding the right title for that book. I found that I was not alone in this searching for the just-right title.

Did you know that Peter Benchley had several titles for his now-famous book before he settled on a final one? *Great White, Shark, The Jaws of Death* and *A Silence on the Water,* to name a few. Do you know the final title? *Jaws,* of course. Would a different title have made a difference? I think so.

What difference would it have made if Steig Larsson had called his first book *The Swedish Girl* instead of *The Girl with the Dragon Tattoo*? It doesn't have quite the same ring, does it? So, it seems that in these days of online book-buying, at the very least, the title of a book does make a difference. Titles do matter, so what was I to do with this title I was so attached to?

Before the second editorial review, I thrashed it out with my trusty reader—the person who has suffered through every single book manuscript for every type of book I've written over the years – my long-suffering husband. Genius that he is—and with a more objective view of the story than the author who had lived with her characters for several years—he suggested the new one, *Grace Note,* I added the sub-title, and I went with it.

The book had a new title that the editor and I both loved, and that would be proudly displayed on the fabulous cove—if we could just agree on the book cover design (which, in the end, I did not like). Before I leave the subject of book titles, though, I would caution you against the advice that seems to be surfacing online these days. It is this: some pundits suggest that you go on a site like Amazon, search for related titles, and see what comes up in the automated search bar suggestions. Bingo! You've got your title that can be found by "millions" of readers. The problem here is that the title may have little to do with the book's actual content, which is misleading for readers—not to mention just plain crackpot. Although, I do have to say that it might work for finding some keywords for a sub-title. Just a suggestion.

What's in a book cover?

Some years ago, I came to a full understanding of the realities of book covers. The book was called *Patient Power! The Smart Patient's Guide to Health Care*. I had written it with my favourite (and only) co-author, my husband Art. I provided the health science communication and writing chops to the collaboration; he offered the medical perspective and the credibility for a health-related book (he's a physician). We were pleased with the manuscript and the editing process. We had agreed on a book title that our editor at the publishing house also liked. Then we were faced with the cover issue.

With previous experience of this publisher, I was armed with all the arguments I could generate about the importance of a persuasive cover that would draw potential readers into it—that would compel them to pick it up off the shelf in a bookstore (that was before most of us browsed the titles online—but research shows that covers are even more critical in the digital book-buying world). That previous experience resulted from this same publisher publishing one of my earlier books with a cover that resembled nothing less than the flag of some unknown nation—neither did it reflect even in the remotest way, what the book was about. They were planning something similar. I could feel it. I shouldn't have been surprised though. The publisher was the University of Toronto Press, and their experience with books for the general public (which this was) was minimal. They were used to dealing with academic tomes but wanted to break into the trade market. They were unlikely to do it with the cover designs to date.

My husband and I flew to Toronto to meet with the art director because we had somehow convinced the editor-in-chief that a more personalized cover, perhaps with the two of us on it, might be more appealing to people interested in their health and decisions about it. We were in for a pleasant surprise.

We took a taxi to a studio in an old brownstone in the heart of the city. It didn't look like much from the outside, but on the inside, the place was an amazing photo studio. But what was more impressive was the art director himself.

New to the position, he'd been with the press for only a few months. As we chatted, it was clear that we were on the same page, as they say. I knew this when he shared his opinion about a cover he had recently created for another of UTPs' books.

"I could have photocopied the book and sent copies to all twelve of the people who were likely to read it," he said with some irony.

His disdain for obscure academic publications was apparent, and I feared for his career's longevity with this esteemed press but was heartened nonetheless. Perhaps we'd get more than a few coloured lines across a cover with a mundane typeface this time around. We did.

The cover was dynamite, and the blow-up of it looks fantastic on my home-office wall. But I learned lessons about the importance of the visual impact of covers, which brings me back from the late 1990s into the twenty-first century.

A few years ago, when my memoir was in the process of being published, my publisher sent me a mock-up of the cover she was suggesting, as publishers do. I had developed more discernment and pickiness about my covers over the years, and in my view, the cover she offered didn't even reflect what the book was about. It was related but seriously misleading. *What in the world is wrong with publishers*? I thought. Clearly the cover designer had not read the book—perhaps not even the blurb.

A story of my journey as the mother of an elite ballet dancer who happened to be a boy, the book begged for a cover reflecting something of a boy's life in dance, or at least of a ballet mom. What she sent me was a photo of a ballerina's foot—on pointe! Did the cover designer not even know that boys don't wear pointe shoes? It seemed clear that the cover designer didn't know what the book was about beyond its setting in the ballet world.

I asked my son, who, in addition to being a dancer, also happens to be a talented photographer, if he might consider taking a photo for the cover. He was delighted to help, and we ended up with a terrific cover in the end. It was one my publisher and I both liked.

What's in a cover?

With all the effort that seems to go into book cover design, it's central to review the answer to one fundamental question: How important is your book cover? In a word: very. *Smashwords* founder Mark Coker is quoted as saying: "Our brains are wired to process images faster than words…When we see an image, it makes us feel something." He is also of the opinion that there is a clear connection between a book's cover and its sales potential. And he does know a thing or two at this stage about what sells books.

There is little hard data about this issue. Still, anecdotal evidence suggests that a book cover can make or break your sales—whether you are published traditionally or are doing it yourself. But how do we ensure that our covers are professional, appropriate and dynamic?

First, we need to agree that book covers can either tempt potential readers or repel them. If you believe that it is only the book blurb copy that draws them in, you need to understand that a large part of how we take in information is visual, and those book covers, even the tiny ones on the online sites, are so critical.

You might think that publishing with a traditional publisher would practically guarantee a dynamite cover. As my story above illustrates, this may not be the case. However, when your publisher (or the book cover designer you hire to create a cover for your self-published book) consults with you about a cover, do you really have any idea what you should be looking for? Do you know what the cover needs to look like to appeal to your target readers? You can't rely entirely on your gut for this.

In "Anatomy of a Book Cover" *Writer's Digest* provides a list of the elements that all go together to create a cohesive whole that can either interest or deter your potential readers. These elements are as follows:

- *Cover imagery.* Imagery can comprise illustration, photography or graphics. Different kinds of books need different types of imagery. Obviously, the imagery on the cover should relate to the book's genre and story. Nonfiction books will often have covers with only graphics on them, but this seems to be less optimal for fiction. Does the image draw a reader in? Does it pull in readers who are interested in your genre? On the other hand, could it be misleading?

- *Typography.* Typography comprises the words on the cover and the typeface(s) in which the words are rendered. In this mix, you have to consider the typeface's size(s). If, for example, you are an unknown writer, it doesn't make sense for your name to be the most prominent element on the cover. The title ought to be larger. However, if you are a best-selling author with a considerable following, your name might more reliably draw in the reader than the new title. And on the subject of typefaces: this is one of the places where an amateurish cover really stands out. If you don't know anything about font types, now is the time to go online and learn something about it. Fonts have both purpose and feel. For example, Serif fonts are more readable for large chunks of text (not a cover consideration but an interior design consideration) than sans serif fonts (if you don't know what these are, stop now and go look them up). Also, some kinds of fonts are romantic, while others are childish. Some evoke a contemporary vibe, while others seem to draw you into the past. You want to ensure that you use the right font. And make sure you use no more than two different fonts on the cover—perhaps one for the title, another for the sub-title and the author's name. Oh, and no matter how much you like how it looks, make sure that it is legible.

- *Spine and back cover*: Although these are strictly issues for print books, spines and back covers are no less important. Consider this: if your potential readers are online where you have maximized the appeal and visibility of your cover and posted that terrific blurb, you have that covered. However, what if your potential readers are browsing actual, brick-and-mortar bookstores? What will entice them to buy your book? The first thing they may see is the spine. Does the title stand out? Is it easily readable? Is the colour appealing? Then, your potential fan pulls the book off the shelf, and what does he or she do next? The future fan immediately looks at the cover, then—you guessed it—turns it over. On the back cover, you'll need that blurb, presented in a visually readable and appealing way. You might even have an author photo if that is likely to entice readers further.

Whether you write fiction or nonfiction, your cover is your number one marketing tool regardless of sub-genre. Ignore it at your peril.

The genesis of a book cover

As you can see from my own tales from the book-cover trenches, it does not matter how the book is being published. As the author, you will have to be involved on some level in book promotion in general and cover design in particular.

If you are self-publishing, you have a very important responsibility to yourself and your readers to consider how you'll get from the book cover concept to the final graphic execution. Writing in the *New Yorker*, Tim Kreider put it this way: "Getting to design your own book cover is the sort of ultimately maddening power that probably shouldn't be entrusted to vain mortals." Who are those mere mortals? That would be you and me.

In general terms, writers are not designers, although if you do happen to be a professional designer, you have a tremendous skill that will now come in handy. It will be useful when you argue with the designers and marketers at your traditional publishing house. If you are self-publishing and are not a professional graphic designer, you need help. Some of us need more help than others. The difficulty comes when you don't realize how ghastly your cover really is when you insist on doing it yourself. And it has been my observation recently that posting your cover on a Facebook writers' group is likely to garner you more positive than negative feedback regardless of how truly awful it might be. I am often tempted to post a really dreadful mock-up that breaks all the rules just to see how many people say, "Love the cover," "Cool!" or the worst response, "Awesome!" Awesomely appalling! They are hardly the ones you want weighing in on your cover. So, how do you get that cover designed for you?

There is a whole cottage industry out there in the online world of designers who are desperate to design your cover. If you insist on doing it yourself, you do need to know how to use Photoshop® (this is the minimum I insist on) and have a subscription to a source for stock photography. You could also try an online platform such as Canva, which might help move you in the right direction.

Writer's Digest suggests the following considerations for a good book cover design:

- ✓ *Easy-to-read titles*. Remember, the book is more frequently going to be purchased online than in a bookstore these days. The title should probably be larger than you planned (unless, as we discussed above, you have a high degree of personal name recognition), and it should be in a font with high readability: no fancy scripts that readers can't make out.

- ✓ *Keep the text simple*: Stick to no more than two or three (at the absolute most) fonts, avoid boxed graphics entirely. (*Writer's Digest* calls these "T-shirt" designs.)
- ✓ *Keep the colours simple*: Don't use colour gradients or any lurid colours. These kinds of colours look "freakish" rather than eye-catching no matter how much you personally feel they grab a reader. Trust me on this.

- ✓ *Use professional artwork*: Avoid your children's artwork, your own attempts or cheap clip art. There are many sites these days where you can register and use professional photography and graphics. Just remember to cite the source if and as they request. I personally like Pixabay.

✓ *Consider how the cover will look as a thumbnail.* This small size is how most of your potential readers will see your graphic. There's no point in having a lot of sub-title text that no one can read. And remember that some online publishing platforms have rules about what type can and cannot be on the cover and how it has to match the information you enter about the book, which becomes the book's metadata.

I'd add the following: *Make sure the cover art actually reflects what the book is about.*

Be honest even in your visual presentation.

Regardless of how you publish your book or its format, the cover design and execution are critical. Now we need to consider the traditional approaches to book promotion as well as the twenty-first-century additions.

NINETEEN

Tried and True, or Old and Obsolete: Traditional Tools for Book Promotion

"The first page sells this book. The last page sells your next book."
~ Mickey Spillane

BOOK PROMOTION IS NOTHING NEW. Mickey Spillane may have been half right: the last page probably will sell the next book, but before a reader even sees the first page of your book, that reader needs to know it exists. In today's world of too-much-information, your book needs to get in front of potential readers so that they can actually go to that first page. Authors and publishers have been engaged in this often frustrating business for centuries, and some long-standing tools and tactics have been used again and again—for better or for worse.

The following traditional tools and tactics for book promotion form this chapter's focus: the book launch, the author tour, the author reading, author photos and bios, news releases, media kits and book reviews. We'll also briefly examine the role that entering writers' contests might or might not play in using the more traditional tools to market your book.

Author photos and bios: Reasons to care

They say a picture is worth a thousand words, but I'm wondering what those thousand words could possibly be as I contemplate the photos on some of the covers of books on my own bookshelf. Then, when I read the authors' bios, I notice that the author bio issue is even more fraught.

Generally, from my point of view, the author photo on the book cover has two distinct objectives:

- To assist in the marketing of the book, and
- To massage the author's ego.

Achievement of the first objective is challenging to figure out. Achievement of the second is a lot easier.

Book marketers see the potential book buyer's visual needs as very important (that's why covers are so important, as we have already discussed). Thus, the author's photo is a key part of the book jacket's appeal or lack thereof as far as they're concerned. Remember that even if your book is only electronic, this photo will likely appear somewhere online. There are several good reasons to care about your photos.

Believe it or not, your photo may actually help to sell your books. Readers often like to think of the author as someone like them or, at least, as a real person. Your photo is part of your brand recognition that you may see value in building. This identification is especially true if you are a series writer.

If you are writing nonfiction in particular, the photo can also be significant. But beware: how you present yourself visually can either add to or take away from your authority and credibility in your field. For example, if you are writing about style and fashion, a reader will be able to trust your work more if you look as if style and fashion are important to you. If you are a physician writing about health and healthcare, you need to look the part.

However, the bottom line is that **no one really knows the extent to which an author's image assists in the selling of the book**. No one seems to have done any substantial research.

Paul Hiebert, writing online in *Flavorwire* some years ago, made a very good point when he said, "Excellent authors avoid writing clichés. The problem is that some of these very authors do not apply the same level of vigilance when it comes to taking promotional photographs, whether they're for magazine profiles or back-of-the-book biographies..." He describes the kinds of staged photos that really do give little information to the potential reader and often make the author look, well, clichéd.

If you think that no one looks at author photos, you may well be wrong. According to David Wills' piece with the catchy title "The Curse of the Douchey Author Photo," people *do* seem to notice. He relates a story of writing an email to a reader who had the audacity to write a nasty note about his author photo. It makes an author think carefully about image, and both the picture and the bio influence image and personal brand. My number one recommendation: do not troll your social media accounts to find that gem your best friend took that weekend when you all got drunk. Just don't do it.

Over the years, I've had publishers who insisted that there be no author photo (very hard on the author's ego) and others who insist on one (easy on the ego if I get to select the photo—which I insist upon). Their larger focus was on the author bio.

A succinct statement of author credentials is important to readers who are looking for information in addition to entertainment. Background on the author is especially important to readers of nonfiction. I take great pains over the construction of that *very brief* bio, considering the needs and wants of the actual target market. What do they want to know about me? What do *I* want them to know about me? What do I *not* want them to know about me? What do they *need* to know about me? What do they not care about? Then I avoid over-sharing – the plague of the modern technological society.

When it comes to fiction, the author's bio might not be all that important. As a reader, do you care what kinds of previous books the author wrote? Possibly. Especially if that author has written many similar books. But as the author, you probably do care that your readers know about other books you have written. That's why you will list those in the actual book itself. Do you care where the author lives? Probably not. But you might be interested to know if the author lives in the UK versus the US. You will probably be more concerned about the book blurb on the cover and whether it is compelling to you as an individual reader. Do you care what the author looks like? Unlikely. But you might be curious. The real downside to this is that an author photo might actually put off the bigots of the world, who might be the very people who need to open their minds. Potential readers' preconceived notions about writers can be a double-edged sword of which to be careful. These are some of the reasons why it's important to consider who your target readers are when creating that book marketing plan.

Media releases and kits: Pivotal or pointless?

Press releases, the nomenclature of old, and their accompanying press kits are intimately tied to the traditional notion of publicity generation. Today's press is no longer really a "press" in the conventional sense—that is print media—rather, we are dealing with the more general media, both traditional and new. Media, with access to many readers/viewers/listeners, is a world that you need to enter to market your book. Knowing how to communicate with media is key to generating publicity in this arena.

First, what are media releases and what is a media kit? These are bedrock public relations tools that still have value even in the twenty-first century's digital world. I've taught many students to develop these tools and have developed my own definitions over the years.

> A **media release** is a one-page news announcement created using the traditional journalistic, inverted-pyramid structure summarizing the who, what, when, where and why of the news in the first paragraph followed by the complete story. Most media (or news) releases end with a boiler-plate statement.*

> A **media kit** is a package of materials—either in print or more commonly these days, electronic format—that includes the following pieces: a cover letter, a media release, a backgrounder feature, a list of frequently asked questions, a list of important bulleted points. It may also contain samples. In the case of book kits, this sample is an excerpt.

*[A boilerplate statement is copy about you, the author, that can be used with few if any changes on all promotional materials. Organizations always have these statements at the end of media releases to provide consistent background.]

Media releases and kits are important because the traditional media, and even the new media (such as book bloggers), still act as gatekeepers for what is publicized. Thus, as an author who wants to sell books, you need to get your book in the right public's eye. Whether you are self-publishing and need to create or contract out the development of these materials for yourself or have a traditional publisher with a marketing department, understanding how important these are will help you communicate with the media.

Over the years, I have filled out numerous marketing forms for my publishers. These forms are long and tedious to complete. Still, they are just about the only way that a traditional publisher's marketing department can develop media releases and other materials to generate publicity. If you are faced with one of these forms, take it seriously and spend some time considering what you'll write and how you will write it. Typical questions on the form are as follows:

- Author background (this is especially important in a nonfiction book where you're presented as an expert)
- List of previous publications
- A 150-word bio
- Subject category for your book
- Short description (maximum 250 characters)
- Longer description (250 words), which becomes the basis of the copy attached to it on web sites etc.
- Important features of the book. (For nonfiction, this might include resource lists, worksheets etc. For fiction, you might have a book club reading guide or the first chapter of your next book at the end.)
- Keywords (they will use these to tag the book online, so you should spend some time thinking about this and doing some online research).
- The market: Who will buy this book?
- A list of places you think will/might review the book
- Your personal media contacts, if any

- Your online presence (an author Facebook page, your Twitter handle, your blog, your Instagram feed etc.)

As you can see, answering these questions is akin to fleshing out a marketing plan. If you are self-publishing, you would be wise to consider all of these elements on your own. Of course, the media releases and materials are entirely useless if you create them without a plan to disseminate them. If you go back to your marketing plan, as we discussed earlier, you'll begin to see how all of these elements fit together like pieces of a puzzle.

Pivotal or pointless? Pivotal, I think.

The traditional book launch

When I held my first book in my hand all those years ago and looked at the cover, I had so many expectations. I recall thinking that a book launch ought to "launch" the book into the marketplace. Sounds reasonable, doesn't it? However, traditional book launches for an unknown writer's work have a limited capacity to generate publicity. This limitation is defined by the number of people who attend and their connections. The real purpose of the book launch is this: *to celebrate a singular accomplishment*.

I've had a few book launches in my day. My first book launch consisted of a reception at a hotel with numerous guests. Oh, I forgot to mention—unless your name starts with "O" and you have no need for a last name, you will probably have to pay for that book launch yourself, whether you self-publish or are taken on by a traditional publisher. A traditional publisher published my first book, and I assure you that I paid for the launch party—although the publisher flew in for it on her own dime. You'll talk about your book and perhaps even read from it if anyone wants to listen. You'll sign and sell a few books (or give them away, as I mentioned in an earlier chapter), but remember that it's really a party.

My favourite book launch happened a few years ago when I launched my memoir *Another Pointe of View: The Life and Times of a Ballet Mom* (Dreamcatcher Publishing). The most personal of all the books I've ever written (or am likely to write in the future), the book tells the story of my journey on the periphery of the world of the elite ballet dancer. As I mentioned along the way, the ballet dancer in my life happens to be my son.

I knew that I'd like to celebrate the book, so I had to find a way to interest people beyond my family and closest friends, or I'd be preaching to the choir. That's when it struck me: if they won't come to learn about a book (not a lot of people actually attend book launches as a part of their regular social calendar), I knew that they'd come if I invited a professional ballet dancer that many people in the community knew. Thus, I convinced my son (who was at the time dancing with the National Ballet of Canada) to get on an airplane, bring along a colleague and dance for us at home—something that he had not done since his early training because he left home (which was on the east coast of Canada at that time) to attend Canada's National Ballet School at the age of eleven.

On that beautiful spring day, Mother's Day to be exact (a book about mothering seemed a brilliant fit time-wise), they danced for us, and I filled an auditorium to watch and listen to me read from my book. I knew that most of them had come to see him dance, but I was fine with that. I had a captive audience!

A successful book launch just takes a bit of creative planning—and a willingness to pay the bills yourself.

Author tours are fun!

When I think back over the years through all of the books of different genres that I've published, I realize that I've accumulated much experience and understanding of book promotion. There are many things that authors themselves can and should (and need to) do to promote their books, but the truth is that since that first book of mine was published so many years ago, everything has changed. With the advent of social media and online conversations, all bets are off, and the tried and true methods for book promotion will never be the same.

That said, at the time when my first book was published, I had a romantic notion of the author tour. When my publisher told me that there would, indeed, be a tour, I was delighted—it would be my fifteen minutes of fame. So, off I went to points west (since I lived on the east coast, everything was west) to be wined and dined and toured. Well, there was actually no wining and dining, but there were publicists who picked me up at hotels and took me to media interviews. It was such fun.

I talked to print journalists who took photos and wrote bits and pieces; I did live television interviews; I did remote television interviews (where you speak into a camera lens as if you were in the studio talking to the interviewer all the while with an earpiece that threatens to fall out); I did radio shows.

I flew to Vancouver first, and a publicist hired by my publisher immediately whisked me off to two television interviews. As you may recall, my first book was about organ transplantation and was somewhat controversial since I didn't just worship at the feet of the transplant surgeons whose God-like presence saved lives. I asked questions about the ethics of some of the decisions the team members made and how they made them. It made great television to pit this lone health writer with real experience in the transplant business against the powerful medical establishment. It's a good thing that even unwelcome and unplanned controversy can promote a book.

Then I was off to Toronto for more television, radio and print interviews. We skipped the smaller media markets to save money on the author tour—for which my publisher paid.

But the question we need to ask today is this: Was it useful and worth the expense to do this kind of book tour as publicity (fun notwithstanding)? I'm not sure. There's little doubt that you can generate publicity for this kind of nonfiction book this way, but the publicity machine has changed dramatically since that time, and all the rules and vehicles have been transformed.

According to Noah Charney, writing in *The Atlantic* in 2016, the book tour really died with the 2008 recession. As publishers tightened their belts, the book tour, it seems, was the first casualty. That's probably because there has never been any objective way to measure this traditional marketing tool's return-on-investment. Today, authors on tour are much more likely to be big-name draws. These are usually people like Michele Obama and Oprah Winfrey whose names draw crowds—usually paying crowds.

These days, the truth of the matter is that readers seem to be drawn to books less by the traditional media machine than they are by word-of-mouth recommendations. And much of this WOM comes not really in person but via social media contacts, friends and followers. Couple this with our individual inclinations to search for our personal interests online, and our book choices come from tailored recommendations for us. And you know that in these days of social media, it is all about "me"—for better or for worse. It could probably be said that the "blog tour" is a modern-day version of the traditional book tour, but I have no experience whatsoever with these tools—either as an author or a reader, so I can't comment on them at all.

Author readings: Are they worth the effort?

Someone recently asked me if I'd consider taking part in an author reading event featuring my newest book. If someone had asked me this question twenty years ago when I first started shopping books to publishers, I would have been flattered. I would have jumped at the chance. However, many years of writing and publishing experience have left me a bit dubious about these events. And discussing these kinds of events with other writers does little to disabuse me of the notion that they are mostly a waste of time—depending on your objective. So, what precisely are the possible objectives of an unknown author reading in public?

From a publisher's point of view (and you personally, if you are both writer and publisher), there is only one bottom line objective: the bottom line. The objective has to be to sell more books. Publishers seem to believe that putting an unknown author in front of twenty people will result in massive book sales. I have no idea where they got that idea. Given the effort involved in doing a reading and the sales potential from such a small audience, one has to question the wisdom of this approach. Keep in mind, though, that there is no effort on the publisher's part—only on the part of the writer and the organizers, often bookstores.

From the writer's perspective, if you are a well-known author, the audience will come in droves to meet you and wait in line for you to sign their books. The point here is that your audience will mostly comprise people who already know you or your work. If, however, you are an unknown writer, the effort involved for you to participate in this kind of event might not be equal to the outcome: you are likely to work a lot harder than it's worth in the end. So, do it only if you love these things.

From a reader's perspective, it's a free evening (or afternoon) of entertainment. Usually, there are refreshments; often, there will be like-minded people attending. Sometimes readings are at bookstores; sometimes, they're in libraries or other related public spaces. When I was in New York City one July, I visited an enormous bookstore on Broadway where they had a more or less permanent dais and chairs set up for readings. Only in a large city would you ever see this. But, is an author reading really "entertainment"?

My most recent experience of doing a reading was at a "literary festival" where several authors would take part in workshops and do readings. This particular afternoon, when I was scheduled to read from my memoir (it was about one-month pre-publication at the time), I was on the agenda after three others reading from their varied recent books. What can I say? At the risk of being scolded by fellow authors, my only conclusion that (painful) afternoon was that writers are crappy speakers. To say I was appalled would be an understatement. One after the other, they took to the stage and monotonously read, sounding ever so slightly like a hostage forced to read a statement on camera. *Every single one of them was cringe-worthy.* It was all I could do to stay awake.

Every fall, the season of author readings is ushered in by publishers. At the beginning of one such season a few years ago, Douglas Bell, writing in the *Globe & Mail*, offered us a piece aptly titled: "The season of readings is upon us, let the misery begin." I was delighted to note that I am not the only one who cringes at the thought of authors reading from their work. Bell quotes Irish author Aidan Higgins. He says it so much better than I can:

> "There's nothing more calculated to cause a gritting of the teeth, a shudder of the spirit or even a rising of the gorge than to be voluntarily confined in a Function Room to endure an hour-long ranting by the author in person, of predigested matter now regurgitated, delivered in a monotonous drone. It is enough to make a cat laugh or a dog throw up."

(I beg you to read the article, which is listed in the sources at the end of the book. If it doesn't make you laugh out loud, you have even less of a sense of humour than I do.)

I've been teaching and doing public speaking for many years. I've taken the time to hone my skills, and it was clear when I came to the podium and began talking about my writing, then read from my book, that this was a breath of fresh air for the audience. You can just tell when they wake up. But sell books? The outcome is limited.

When you spend so much solitary time with your work as writers do, I think it can be fun to share it with a live audience however, if you are a rotten speaker, just back away. Please. The fact is that unless you're a celebrity, to begin with, or have a rabid following from previous books, the reading will not sell many books in any case. And if you already are a celebrity or have a fan base, they're going to buy the book anyway. So, the reason for doing it has to be more than just selling books.

So, here are my tips for doing an author reading:

- *Don't focus on selling books.* Just focus on connecting with live people and having some fun.
- *Prepare in advance.* Take the time to consider what you'll say to put your reading into context for the audience. Select the passage you plan to read carefully.
- *Consider your presentation skills.* If you're not a good presenter and can't make your work come alive for the audience, either get some coaching or just don't do it.
- *Practice your remarks and your reading.* Do this out loud and listen to yourself.
- *For the love of God, don't drone on and on.* Or you'll have to carry a gun – to put the audience out of their misery.

When is a book review not a book review?

There is little doubt that book reviews fall into the tried-and-true category of book promotion and marketing. That said, this discussion could just as easily come under the topic of the next chapter: *Shiny & New*, because the way book reviews are handled these days is most often a direct result of the new approach to digital book marketing. But let's begin our discussion with the question of whether or not book reviews these days are even helpful.

A traditional book review was (and sometimes still is) written by a book reviewer for a news outlet. Occasionally, the reviewer receives a copy of the book, and sometimes the media outlet pays for it. Either way, the reviewer is merely doing the job for which the media outlet pays him or her: a five-star review will not pay more than a one-star review, so there is some journalistic motivation, to be honest. These kinds of reviews were third-party endorsements at their most objective. However, since book reviews have become part of the algorithm that online book sellers like Amazon use to rank books and give them a higher spot in searches, book reviews are fraught with myriad problems in the age of digital book publishing and sales.

It seems simple enough. You write a book, someone reads it, likes it (or not), posts an honest review, and other potential readers interpret the review for themselves, deciding whether or not to read your book based on their own criteria. It seems simple enough. It is not.

One of the essential factors readers might use to interpret a review is the identity—and therefore perceived credibility—of the review writer.

These days, there is a big difference between a review written by the *New York Times* and one penned by Oprah (or at least endorsed by her). Or between the writer's spouse and someone who doesn't know that writer personally. That may be the line we cross into territory where a review is not really a review—it is an advertisement. And these are not the only kinds of advertisements masquerading as book reviews.

There can hardly be a writer or wannabe writer around these days unaware of the current book review scams visited upon readers.

In August 2012, *The New York Times* published an article titled: "The Best Book Reviews Money Can Buy." In one of the first exposés of the phenomenon, which has only worsened since then, author David Streitfeld reported on what appeared to be a newly established business model: writing book reviews for cash. He told the story of Todd Rutherford's gettingbookreviews.com, a business based on writing online book reviews paid for by the author. One of the service packages he offered at the time was for him to write twenty online book reviews for $499. What could be better? Twenty reviews proclaiming a book to be worthy of five stars, the work of a literary genius. In my view, what would be better would be some honesty.

And Rutherford was merely one among countless businesses that continue to spring up all over the place to provide the same service to writers desperate for sales, with few qualms about the dishonesty or ethics of it all. Quite often, the entrepreneurs offering this service are themselves wannabe writers.

By 2015, Amazon, long a supporter of online consumer reviews of its products, decided to take "legal action against businesses it claims sells fake reviews to third-party sellers," as reported by *The Consumerist* online in September of that year. Amazon was taking on all those review factories (and there are many more today). There was even one called buyazonreviews.com [sic – yes, the "ama" part was missing from the URL] that promised, "…that for $19 to $22 per review it will provide five-star write-ups in a 'slow-drip' manner as to avoid detection by the retailer." Clearly, they knew that what they were doing was wrong on so many levels. Purchasing a five-star review is like lying to your potential readers. A review implies authenticity, which is absent in paid reviews.

But what happens when a reader finds out the truth of the review? Maybe the book is a good one, but maybe it isn't. Readers searching for new, indie writers will soon become jaded from being burned. Buying book reviews hurts everyone.

So, if a book review is not a book review when it is written for money, what about when it's written by your spouse (or mother, or sister, etc.)?

I was mortified when I went onto Amazon.com one day to see that one of the reviews (and a five-star one at that) of one of my historical novels was penned by someone whose last name is PARSONS. I'm quite sure that anyone looking at that would make the reasonable assumption that the author of the review was one of my relatives. It wasn't. I'm just glad the reviewer liked it. However, the bottom line is that a review by one of your nearest and dearest isn't really a review either. There is bias involved.

Here is the one where I land myself in trouble with fellow writers: What if the review is written by a member of your co-dependency group? These are those writing groups, those virtual communities we have explored before in this book (there are many on Facebook as well as on specific websites), wherein everyone gushes about everyone else's books, mostly so that when yours is published, everyone will do the same for you. I have to admit that this bothers me. It puts me off buying the promoted books, which is a shame for the writers. However, I just don't trust these reviews.

I follow several otherwise interesting indie authors who also review books on Twitter, but I find their reviews are always five stars or very close to it. I'm presuming that they only tweet their five-star ones (surely there are books they dislike?), but I'd like to be directed to one that might be a four or even a three-and-a-half-star review so that I can make up my own mind. When everything is "awesome," nothing is "awesome."

Let's get back to some truth in advertising among writers and publishers. Please.

Writers' contests: The good, the bad & the very ugly

One day, I opened my email to find a note from the *Next Generation Indie Book Awards*.

"Congratulations," it read, "…your book has been named a finalist in the GENERAL FICTION/NOVEL (over 80,000 words) category…"

Oh, I thought. What's that? Did I enter that contest? My skepticism kicked in immediately, until I remembered: yes, I did enter this contest many months earlier, when I was fixated on book marketing. But now I found myself researching it again to see if there was any legitimacy to it, and, for that matter, to any of the contests designed to part independent and small-press-published authors from their money (most, if not all, have entry fees).

What's the point of giving awards for books? It used to be—back in the day, as they say—that book awards recognized truly gifted authors whose work has or is destined to make a difference. And these awards had an enormous impact on book sales. Some of the most famous still do. Winning a coveted award like the Booker award, the Pulitzer, or the National Book Award, to name a few, certainly puts books on the reading radar. But what about the plethora of awards that no one has ever heard of? What about those obscure little awards that the winners use to put "award-winning" on their websites and book covers? In addition to the long-standing, celebrated awards, there is an absolute glut of new and often questionable writing awards and contests. Enter them at your peril.

Some years ago, the Science Fiction & Fantasy Writers of America posted a terrific description of awards and award scams on their website. They differentiate between outright scams, contest mills, award mills, and fake contests. The list is long and very dispiriting. But why would a writer enter a contest anyway?

If a traditional publisher publishes your book, that publisher might decide to enter your book in an appropriate award contest. Or not. If your book is independently published, then watch out. You will be vulnerable to every possible attempt to get you to enter a contest. Why would you even consider that, anyway?

In a word: publicity. This enticement is the promise. Your book will be read by others who might, just might, like it. Or at least they might—just might—actually read it. They might like it enough that you might win an award. That could mean some extra publicity for you and your book.

Many other people have researched these contests, so I thought I'd take a slightly different approach. I hypothesized that if a book award is so credible, then the books awarded must be of high quality.

I took a random sample (albeit a convenience sample for all of you researchers out there) to gather some anecdotal evidence to support or discredit my thesis.

I started with one year's worth of Independent Publisher Book Awards, which bills itself as the "World's largest international and regional book awards competition," and selected their first-place winner in the popular fiction category. To gather some information about this book to inform my purchasing decision, I clicked over to Amazon to "read inside the book." This information always helps me to decide if it's a book I'd like to read. I usually look at the front and back covers, the table of contents (this is more important in nonfiction, though), and then read a sample to see if the writing is appealing. At first, I was not aware that this author's first book was *Sideways*, which later morphed into the film of the same name, which might ring a bell for you. The information I gleaned from this research suggested to me that I would likely enjoy the book. He writes in an accessible and entertaining way. It occurred to me that it might just fill my need for summer schlock reading this year.

Next on my list was the Writer's Digest Award for self-published authors. They are a credible organization, charge a substantial entry fee and offer the following: the chance to win cash, national exposure for your work, the opportunity to catch the attention of prospective editors and publishers, and a paid trip to the ever-popular Writer's Digest Conference in New York City. They offer several awards, including ones for self-published books, self-published ebooks and short stories, among others. In all, they hand out somewhere in the vicinity of 500 awards in a variety of categories each year, just in their general writing contest. Needless to say, I have not examined all the winners yet.

From 2008 until 2015, the Amazon Breakthrough Novel Award was a highly visible award for self-published authors. Their prize was a publishing contract with Penguin, with whom they had a partnership. I was impressed by some of their winners back in the day.

I've concluded that the more high-profile of these awards really do have some substance behind them. There will always be scams of which writers must be aware, but in the grand scheme of things, if you do your research, entering a contest like this just might get you what you're looking for—recognition and perhaps a bit of publicity. But beware: there are more scams out there than there are legitimate contests.

Here are my suggestions to unknown authors who are interested in entering their work in book contests:

- ✓ Before doing anything, sit down and decide what your objective is. If it's to get onto the NYT best-seller list, you

might be a wee bit unrealistic. If you want publicity, it's possible. If you'd like a bit more exposure, you'll likely get it. At least your work will be read by someone. If you like the thought of being a "winter" of something, that's okay, too.
- ✓ Decide how much money you're willing or able to spend on entry fees. Most of these contests, even some of the more credible, charge for entries.
- ✓ Do an online search for contests that fit your particular genre, just as you would when seeking a compatible publisher.
- ✓ Select four or five that impress you the most and research them. Explore some of the previous winners in categories that interest you. Look at what bloggers or independent writers are saying apart from what is on the website.
- ✓ Read the contest's website very carefully. Look at every bit of the fine print. Then go to a list of current writing scams and check to see if it is on the list.
- ✓ Decide on one or two contests. Don't waste your money on a whole raft of contests.
- ✓ Read the entry requirements carefully.
- ✓ Follow the instructions to the letter—and make sure your entry is in before the deadline.
- ✓ Then wait.

Oh…and it might be worthwhile to make a note of contests you enter.

TWENTY

Shiny and New, or Ineffectual and Time-Sucking: The New Wave of Promotional Tools

> "*LinkedIn is for the people you know. Facebook is for the people you used to know. Twitter is for people you want to know.*" ~ Source unknown

AMERICAN AUTHOR AND MARKETER Seth Godin has been quoted as saying, "The future of publishing is about having connections to readers and the knowledge of what those readers want." Twenty-first-century connections are usually made via the Web. Whenever I have a new book about to launch, regardless of its provenance (traditional or self-published), I dig out my research skills to see if there is any new actual hard evidence on what really works to sell books. Lately, there's been an excessive amount of material on the need for a (huge) social media presence. It seems to be the collective wisdom that publishers won't touch you with a ten-foot pole if you don't have thousands of Twitter followers, vast numbers of Facebook "friends" or "likes," and more than a foot in Instagram's door. Whether or not this represents the views of a majority of publishers isn't entirely clear. However, it's not only the traditional route to publication that seems to beg for this: there are more blog posts for indie authors on this topic than perhaps any other single current issue. However, as seems to be the ongoing case, there doesn't appear to be any hard data, and data is something that I rely on. I need data to support the need for this extraordinarily time-consuming new requirement.

Nevertheless, there seems to be an almost religious fervour about the "author platform" concept, which is nothing more or less than your reputation and reach both on and offline. Given that very little gets bought or sold these days without the benefit of cyberspace, we'll make the reasonable assumption that, at the very least, the unknown writer who would like to be a known author needs to explore the new world of marketing opportunities.

What is your "platform," and do publishers really care?

Since, as I mentioned above, publishers don't seem to have much in the way of hard data about the value of the new social media approaches to book marketing, we'll begin by looking at an industry that has done at least a modicum of homework here. Some years ago, a colleague tweeted to me a story about a study of the use of social media by charities. The piece titled "Facebook Users Give their 'Likes' – but not their Dollars—to Charities: Study Reports" provides some evidence indicating what "liking" things on social media might really mean. (The report was published in the *Calgary Herald*, but the link to the story is no longer available to be listed in the sources section.)

A Ph.D. student at the University of British Columbia on Canada's west coast studied the correlation between someone "liking" a charity on Facebook and being moved to volunteer or donate. What he found might come as something of a surprise to the more naïve among us. The more likely someone is to click "like," the less likely they are to actually give money. The researchers characterize these people as *slactvitists* – a breed of individual who likes the feeling of publicly supporting a good cause but feels no need to actually do something about it or perhaps considers the act of clicking to be the equivalent of "doing" something. If this is the case in the non-profit industry, arguably, we can extrapolate to the bookselling industry to theorize that the more likely someone is to "like" you on Facebook or "follow" you on Twitter, the less likely that person is to buy your book. Once they've taken this "action," they perhaps feel that they've done enough to support you. It's an interesting argument that has as much foundation as the opposite assumption and maybe more.

Let's take this argument a step further. Wait a minute, you say, even if that's true (and maybe the book's not for them), if they are active on Twitter, for example, then at the very least, they're more likely to tweet about it. This is unlikely, especially if they follow more than a few hundred accounts (studies show that if you follow large numbers of accounts on Twitter, you cannot possibly keep up with their tweets with any degree of regularity). For the sake of argument, though, let's say they do tweet it, and then someone else re-tweets it, and on it goes. If our original premise is correct, none of this matters. Your book can be tweeted all over cyberspace, and it is still a distinct possibility (probability is more like it) that *no one will buy it anyway.* Many indie authors would be millionaires (or at least making a luxurious, regular wage) if this were true. So, we're back where we started.

It seems that the notions of a *platform* and a *social media platform* are distinct but related concepts that need to be differentiated.

It has always been the case that a nonfiction author needs a platform, but that doesn't necessarily mean thousands of Twitter followers. It means the author has the credentials and expertise to write a credible book. You can rest assured that neither my editors nor the reviewers at the academic and professional presses where some of my nonfiction books have been published cared a bit about my online presence in recent years. They did care about my background, education, experiential credentials, and my ability to write authentically, clearly, and correctly. These are still the most important planks in the platform that supports your work.

Those thousands of Twitter followers might also be impressive, but they are at the lower end of what's needed, at least initially. That being said, it's also the case that some agents or editors will look at your social media posts to assess your ability to communicate and to determine if you have some kind of a unique voice and/or point of view. It's probably safe to say that if your social media accounts—especially your blog if you have one—are seriously out of date, this may not bode well.

Literary agent Carly Watters has said, "Twitter is a place for authors—who live a very solitary existence – to engage with other writers going through the same experience, follow industry veterans, follow writers they admire and learn about how the book business works." Note carefully that she did not suggest here that it is a primary marketing tool. Instead, she seems to suggest that Twitter—and it stands to reason other platforms such as Instagram and Facebook—has additional value for writers apart from marketing.

In her excellent post "A definition of author platform," blogger and writing coach Jane Friedman gives us this useful advice: "Your platform should be as much of a creative exercise and project as the work you produce. While a platform can give you the power to market effectively, it's not something you develop by posting "Follow me!" on Twitter or "Like me!" on Facebook a few times a week." This was true when she wrote this in 2011, and it continues to be true today.

So, what might your social media presence be good for?
- Finding beta readers far afield.

- Doing background research and getting tips.
- Learning about writing and the publishing business.
- Finding support from like-minded, unknown writers.

And as for this last bullet, I'm reminded of the phenomenon of co-dependency. Beware.

Author websites: Need to have, nice to have or nuts to have?

So, you've written your first book. Do you really need a personal author website? Probably, but it's worth considering the question of whether it is a need or just nice to have.

J.K. Rowling has an impressive website. It's professional, complete and up-to-date. It's just the kind of website you would expect the creator of the Harry Potter brand, and of late, the Cormoran Strike brand, to have. And I do not doubt that her millions of fans visit it when they need all things JKR. Stephen King's website is different. It's densely packed with information and has a darker quality. It's just what you might expect from him. However, what's the unknown author's point in having a personal website (beyond the obvious ego-massaging aspect)?

If you search online to answer this question, you will be bombarded by a stream of websites proclaiming loudly that you NEED a website. On closer inspection, though, these are mainly websites from organizations that are in the business of creating author websites. Of course, they think you need one, and they want you to hire them to create it. But really? Who will visit it?

In general terms, and in these days of social media, you have to be clear that a web presence is just that—a web *presence*. It is stationary, motionless, more or less fixed, the opposite of dynamic.

A web presence is usually a static site where organizations or people can hang information. If they seek to be dynamic or to engage with others (in the case of authors – presumably your readers), then they need to be *connected* to opportunities for encouraging this engagement: an author blog, a forum of some kind (perhaps a Facebook page where discussion can take place on the "wall"), a wiki (wherein you might engage your readers to help you create a piece of writing – but that's a bit odd in my view, and seems to be out of style anyway).

In 2011, author David Sterry wrote a piece in *The Huffington Post* focusing on Anik LaFarge's interview, the author of *The Author Online: A Short Guide to Building Your Website, Whether You Do It Yourself (and You Can!) or You Work With Pros*. Just as you might imagine, the discussion of the pros and cons is hardly balanced: the interview subject is, after all, in the business of creating author websites, so naturally, she thinks that they fall into my "need to have" category. The one thing she does suggest that seems completely useful is this: there's no point in having a website if you don't use it. I couldn't agree more. I think that the question of using it, though, has two components. First, the author has to use it, and then the readers have to use it. I've struggled with this myself. My own author website has often languished, unloved for long periods of time. When I am busily engaged with other things like writing books, it has been a mere presence. It's time-consuming to keep it up. It is a myth that readers will naturally gravitate toward it.

More recently, writing guru Jane Friedman recommended that you have a website even if you are unpublished. Since she strongly believes that all published writers need a website, she thinks starting early, even before publication, will provide a gentler learning curve.

An author's use of his or her website manifests itself in a couple of activities. First, authors need to ensure that the site has useful information that they regularly update for those potential readers who stumble upon it. Having a blog might be an excellent way to engage readers on your website. Second, the author needs to ensure the website material is accurate and well-written. Third, the author needs to get that website into search engines so that it can be found.

As far as readers are concerned, they need to use it to become engaged with the author, which many authors in days gone by weren't interested in. Times have changed. I suppose readers use authors' websites to get the backstory on current work, find out what's coming up, and get background on the author. Those would be three kinds of content to include in an author's website. However, how often do you, as a reader, visit the website for an author you like?

As a reader, I rarely seek out and visit author websites. I'm not sure how many of you do, either.

As a writer, I think that my website tells certain people that I'm a serious writer and that I have accomplished a few things. Who, though, are those certain people? Agents? Filmmakers? New publishers? I don't know the answer, nor is there any research indicating an answer.

My own website caused me considerable soul-searching. Did I need one? What would be its objective? Who would read it (a bit like the question of who will read your book)? Who will design/maintain/update it? Was it worth it?

It seemed like a no-brainer. These days, whether you're an organization or an individual, if you're not on the web, in some sense, you don't exist. Perhaps that's a bit strong, but it does make a point.

The truth is that an author's website is a place for me to send interested individuals whom I meet at parties, etc., who specifically ask if there's anywhere they can read about me. So, if I meet you at a party and you happen to ask what I do (I usually don't talk about myself unless asked these days), and you're interested enough to ask where you can find out more, I'll probably send you to my website. But do I think thousands of people are visiting it monthly? I'm smart enough about websites to be sure of the answer: NO. I know they're not. Remember, though, even impressive website statistics indicating massive numbers of clicks, which are the only real feedback we have, mean only that people were there. This does not necessarily translate directly into book sales.

Do I really need a Facebook presence? Or does any author, for that matter?

A few years ago, I removed everyone from my Facebook "friends" list except close family. "Why in the world would a writer do such a thing?" you might reasonably ask. And it is no small thing to rid oneself of "friends." It takes time, so you do need to be committed to the task and to why you're doing it.

I was sick of Facebook. Every time I opened my news feed, there among the interesting updates from pages that I've liked was the constant narcissistic stream of consciousness from my so-called friends. And I'd bet my next (day job) paycheque that not one of those people gives a rat's a## about what I'm doing, either. But it's not just that. I have often had to bite my cyber-tongue when I see posts. Of course, I could mute them or simply stop following them, but that really misses the point, doesn't it?

How many times does it need to be said? A Facebook friend is not a friend. A real friend doesn't need to keep in touch on Facebook with public posts of anything and everything. But if I sabotaged my Facebook presence, am I not endangering potential book sales? Isn't this the fear of writers who are on Facebook?

Most book marketing gurus these days suggest that you do, indeed, need a Facebook presence. However, that means you need a *fan page* for your work. Your "friends" on your personal profile page will not buy your books. At least most of them will not. But they might ask for them for free!

The way to begin is to start a fan page and invite your "friends" to become fans, rather than trying to be a friend to all your fans.

I'm a fan of several writers and their fan pages on Facebook. It appears to me that the only writers on Facebook who have a real and compelling presence are those who had a name before they put up their Facebook pages. In other words, if you're already a best-selling writer or public personality of another sort and you put up a fan page on FB, your fans will, indeed, flock to you. However, if you are an unknown writer (as are most writers on Facebook), Facebook can become a great time suck. And make no mistake, many of your so-called fans will be other aspiring writers who simply want you to "like" them back. Engaging with other writers is not engaging with readers.

For years now, I've been trying to find some hard data on the extent to which Facebook (or any other social media platform, for that matter) helps writers build their "brand" and sell books to those readers who might enjoy/need them. Even though everyone and their dog seems to be writing about the need to build your platform, these appeals are long on rhetoric and short on hard data.

The truth is, these days, traditional publishers don't seem to understand that one of their roles is to help the author build an audience for a book they believe in. As we have already discussed, there has always been a certain amount of reliance on authors for their marketing input, and it is *all* on you if you choose to self-publish. However, in this new age of publishing, it is more evident than ever. Building an audience is the purview of each individual author, regardless of the publishing model you use. The platform's strength is a function not only of this presence but also, presumably, of some kind of engagement. That means that those thousands of Twitter followers you do have read and reply to or retweet your messages (or whatever you call doing this on "X" these days). You have thousands of Facebook fans or friends who post to your wall, telling you how troubled they are that your new book won't be out for another month or two. You have thousands of blog followers who regularly post pithy comments to which you respond diligently or who click "like," and you go immediately to your (or even their) blog and tell them that you're happy they stopped by. As blogger and writer, Anne Allen once said, "An author with fifty engaged fans on Twitter is going to be far more effective than one with a thousand detached strangers..." It is much more than merely a numbers game.

If you think about it, we could be spending twice as much time engaging with people who might or might not buy and/or read our books as we do writing. I prefer to be writing—since I am a writer. Equally, though, I do recognize that if anyone is actually to read my writing, they have to find it. It's a matter of balance.

Fauzia Burke, president of a digital publicity and marketing firm specializing in creating awareness for books and authors, wrote a piece for *The Huffington Post* titled "Does Social Media Sell Books?" Burke interviewed a best-selling author's agent – an author who was not, at the time, active on Facebook or any other social media platform. But surely the agent would have some data. Nope.

Here's what this agent said:

> "*...it's critical that no matter how active an author is online, the conversation about them and/or their book must be picked up and carried on by others for it to truly have an impact on sales. It can't be ONLY about the author talking (blogging/tweeting)...*" *and later,* "*...For nonfiction authors with a specific expertise, being out there in the community that has interest in that expertise will most likely be effective in selling their book.*"

Most likely to be effective? Most likely? This conclusion is hardly a ringing endorsement. It's something that seems like a good idea, but the return-on-investment (of time in this instance) just doesn't seem to have legs.

More recently, when book publishers were surveyed about how they saw the future of book marketing strategies, 68% indicated that social media marketing was at the top of the list, despite the lack of data on return-on-investment. Unfortunately, in an era of apparent increasing reluctance on the part of legacy publishers to pay for marketing, it seems that social media marketing tools such as Facebook are only effective if they pay for sponsored ads. Indeed, the more you pay for advertising, even on social media platforms, the less ROI you may see if marketing costs eat up all your profits. This is a lesson for both traditionally published authors and self-published ones. A study report titled "Does Social Media Marketing Actually Sell Books?" illustrated the significance of the problem with this example:

"A boutique publisher with over 2.5 million Facebook fans told me they rarely see more than a 5% response rate to their average posts…when posts focus on pushing sales of a specific book, the response rate is even lower."

It is a myth that there is a bulletproof social media marketing strategy that will sell a million copies of your book. For me, I only have so much time in the day. And to tell you the truth, I'd rather be writing on my blogs or working on two new books than checking out photos of someone's cat hanging upside down from a Christmas tree. But that's just me.

Book trailers: What's the point?

Everyone has an opinion about movie trailers. If the trailer is foisted on you without your consent at the beginning of a movie in a theatre, and it's a genre you hate, you probably don't hold a high opinion of trailers. On the other hand, if you actively seek out movie trailers on sites like YouTube, you're a fan. Of course, many movie trailers show you the only interesting/funny/scary parts of a movie you hope will be interesting/funny/scary, only to find out (after paying to see the film) that those actually were the only interesting/funny/scary bits in the entire movie!

With all of that in mind, I'm reasonably sure that you are not quite as familiar with book trailers. A book trailer is a short video clip that presents a small sample of a book in a format similar to a movie. As a reader, when I first heard about book trailers, I thought that the concept was odd. After all, isn't part of the attraction of reading its ability to trigger readers' own internal imaginative processes to create their own internal visual interpretations of characters, places and environment? At least that's how it works in fiction – nonfiction is perhaps another story.

A book trailer, then, although intended to entice us to buy and read the book, may give the imaginative reader too much outside information about the visuals that a writer wants a reader to develop for him or herself. However, in my view, that depends on the visuals presented and the quality of both the script (even if there is no narration, there has to be an underlying script) and the production.

There are thousands of book trailers around. Just search for "book trailers" on YouTube and see what comes up. And that's just the tip of the iceberg. But the question still remains: Is there a point (or bottom-line enhancement) to this additional element in the book marketer's arsenal?

Although some people plug them as a must-have marketing tool these days, there is still little real evidence to support this claim. Five years ago, I tried to find data to support or discredit the idea of the book trailer as an important marketing tool, but couldn't find anything. This is still the case. In other industries, YouTube videos have been shown to increase sales, but there is no real evidence that this is true in the book-buying industry. It has been reported that potential book buyers are more likely to buy your book if they have seen a trailer (this seems obvious to me). Still, the indication that they are any less likely to buy your book if they have seen a trailer isn't a readily verifiable statistic. We need to keep in mind that there are very few pieces of hard evidence to suggest which tools in the marketing toolbox result in more significant book sales.

It is relatively easy to believe that people will stay on your website longer if you have a video for them to watch, but it has to be said that they have to get to the website first. It is worth noting that *many of those people promoting book trailers as important for book marketing are in the business of creating these trailers*. They are biased. Although they might provide an avenue for improving the visibility of books, there is no real evidence that they are worth the time and money required to produce them—at least not yet. However, it might be worth exploring how different genres and their distinct audiences are inclined to buy a book based on a trailer. Indeed, there may be enough reason to produce one if you're interested in expanding your brand into another medium. Don't discount doing one, but know that you have to drive people to see it for it to be useful, just like any other kind of online marketing. And if you can do this, you already know that videos are among the most shareable of online materials.

I did a bit of empirical (but hardly scientific) research on this question a few years ago. I posted several questions on several book sites to ask these avid readers if book trailers ever influence their book-buying. The general theme of the comments was a resounding "no." However, several responders did suggest that book trailers might influence their selection of nonfiction more strongly than fiction. Perhaps that's because they perceive that a book trailer might provide some information that would help them see what's inside the book, like we used to do when we all browsed bookstores. However, with those nifty "see inside the book" options on web-based bookstores, we already get that experience. Just recently, I tried this again, posting similar questions on sites frequented by writers. No one said they had actually ever purchased a book because of a trailer, but they were intrigued. Perhaps more surprising was the number of those in the very large Facebook group of "authors" who had never heard of book trailers.

As hard as I've tried, I have been unable to unearth any hard statistics on the success (or lack thereof) of book trailers in promoting new books. There are vague references to engaging younger readers, such as teens, through this visual medium on YouTube, and to placing book trailers in movie previews in theatres. However, I would wager a guess that this would likely confuse the audience. Is it a movie? Is it a book? Is it a book being made into a movie? And it would be prohibitively expensive.

In general, the publishing industry has not exactly been on the cutting edge of new marketing approaches. Their lack of being at the forefront has always been the case. When other industries were already embracing electronic everything alongside their online presence, book publishers lagged behind.

That lag in the bookselling industry never surprised me, given my thirty-plus years of experience as an author within the traditional publishing industry. These days, study after study supports the contention that web-based marketing is an effective strategy for most products (especially for youth). We can conclude that books are not so different. However, if you couple that with our previous discussion of how books are more often than not purchased through person-to-person recommendations, you can see that a web-based strategy that uses personal connection platforms could be effective. That's probably sufficient rationale for using web-based marketing, but it still doesn't support book trailers *per se.*

Publisher John Wiley and Sons, a well-known and large publisher of professional and academic books, was one of the first to use videos to promote books. They created a series of videos to support their business and personal development titles and posted them on YouTube. This might be the reason that one of the responders to my informal survey indicated that she might buy a nonfiction book based on viewing a book trailer, while another one said that she didn't even know there were book trailers for fiction. There are.

The frustrating thing about the issue of book trailers is that although they're fun (and relatively easy to produce, although creating a high-quality trailer requires talent and skill, and usually money), there is no evidence that they actually contribute materially to the success of a book in the marketplace. Are they cost-effective? Probably not so much. However, publishers seem to point to a book trailer's relatively low cost as part of an essential online publicity campaign, regardless of its effectiveness. A self-publisher needs to bear in mind that trailers are only low-cost relative to the vast sums of money the large publishers are worth. You might find the cost excessive. And it is better to have no book trailer than a crappy, amateurish one.

Five ways your social media platform might be turning toxic

At least twice a week, I seem to acquire new Twitter followers who themselves boast over 10,000 followers. Imagine that! 10,000+

followers! I always surf over to see my new followers' profiles and never cease to be astounded by these huge numbers. But before I click to "follow" back, I always hesitate in these instances. I always seem to have the same question for myself: "Why in the world would I want to follow someone (or some organization) with that many followers unless I'm looking for their information. They certainly won't be interested in anything I have to say. Dear God, they'll never be able to find it!" And I'm left wondering how anyone can possibly be in a balanced give-and-take situation when so many hangers-on are involved.

Throughout my career in the real world and in academia, I've specialized in two areas, one of which is strategy. In that capacity, I've helped hundreds of students develop successful promotional plans for non-profits and small businesses and was an early adopter of social media, teaching our first undergraduate course in the new applications some years ago. It's funny now that I'm looking at my own promotional work, I'm struck by some oddities in the world of social media—and authors.

A social media platform no doubt supports sales of independently published books, as we've already discussed. However, there are a few caveats, the most important of which is that there needs to be some recognition of the point of diminishing returns. I submit that *there is a point at which a writer's online social media presence morphs from supportive and beneficial to toxic*. So, here are some symptoms of toxicity that I've observed.

You might be developing social media toxicity if...

...you find yourself falling victim to groupthink. It's so easy to retweet mindlessly, to give a thumbs-up to any inane post on your Facebook writers' group page, to find yourself nodding in support of ideas that you hadn't given enough time to figure out on your own. I've noticed that, except for the odd outlier, most reply tweets are supportive, and I even find myself falling into this trap, ignoring the tweets that I think are just plain stupid. And note that on Facebook, Instagram and even LinkedIn, there is no "dislike" button. Don't you sometimes feel you'd like to hit that one? (People do it often enough on YouTube.)

…you have an over-inflated notion of how many books you should be selling based on your number of followers, friends, etc. I have to refer back to our earlier discussion about the research supporting the notion that online "likes" don't translate into behaviour.

… you fall victim to that co-dependency problem. Co-dependency is known in mental health circles as relationship addiction, excessive social or emotional reliance on another person who often has a problem. I'm suggesting that writers who toil in isolation often look for support among other writers who understand them, which begins the cycle. Over-dependence can become toxic, leading to inertia and the next symptom of toxicity…

… your social media activities become a major time suck. This can happen so easily; you hardly notice it happening. It's like several of my former students suggested one day in class: they find themselves spending inordinate amounts of time on assignments as a result of keeping their electronic devices at their elbow and responding to every "ping" as texts and tweets arrive. My advice: just turn them off!

…finally, when your admiration is seriously misplaced. I'm talking about the odd phenomenon of actual best-selling writers like Sheila O'Flanagan having fewer Twitter followers (and wisely following far fewer, yet selling books by the millions) while some indie authors who have sold a few thousand (or even hundreds) books have hundreds of times more. It might be worth the unknown writer's (like me) time to follow the ones who have been on the real best-seller lists. Maybe we could learn a thing or two.

So, you might conclude that I'm just sour because I have relatively few Twitter followers. But I'm not. I might have been at one time when I thought that those followers might truly be interested in my work, buy my books and retweet to other actual buyers about my work. But that rarely happens in reality. It's a bit like a viral video: You can't *plan* to use one for promotional and marketing purposes because you have no way of knowing if a video you produce will catch fire or not.

As important as an online platform may well be, perhaps we ought to consider spending less time on our social media presence and more time on our writing.

TWENTY-ONE

Permission to write: Granted by You and Your Future

"A word after a word after a word is power." ~ Margaret Atwood

WHAT DOES THE FUTURE HOLD? Suppose we had a book publishing crystal ball. In that case, I'm afraid all we'd be able to see is a misty future where exciting innovation often runs smack into the face of traditional opinion. Occasionally, we might be able to see that more and more often, the lines between what we now think of as traditional publishing models and the new age of self-publishing begin to blur as hybrid models develop and hybrid authors emerge as a result of either desire or necessity, or both. Both of these have already happened to me, and I expect that both scenarios will play a part in my own writing and publishing ventures in the future. And probably in yours as well.

Books in transition

It may come as a surprise to unknown writers who are feverishly trying to find traditional publishers and even to those who are stalwart adherents of the self-publishing approach. And it happens more often than you might think. It has happened to me more than once, although I'm happy to say that not as often as it hasn't! Here is the surprise: publishers go out of business for one reason or another.

The backstory: Like most serious, albeit unknown, writers out there, I had always gravitated toward traditional publishers. They have the experience. They have expertise. They have money. Perhaps this last one is not a given. In any case, until recent years, it was the only route to being taken seriously as an author, although by this point in our exploration of publishing, it should be clear to you that this is *still* sometimes the case.

Nevertheless, on almost a dozen occasions, I went through the long, drawn-out process of querying, waiting, submitting, waiting, reviewing, waiting, editing, waiting, and so it goes. Eventually, the books saw the light of day, and I moved on. But what happens to your property (your book that you slaved over for a chunk of your life) when your publisher ceases to publish? Notwithstanding the legal issues of who owns the copyright (you should), here's one of my stories.

In 2008, I finally found a publisher for my memoir. The book didn't really do very well despite good reviews. The publisher was not into electronic publishing at all, so it was never available as a downloadable ebook, effectively cutting off a significant and increasingly large proportion of the potential readership even then. The publisher sent me 100 books I did not order, which sat untouched in my office for several years. I'm just not one of those people who are prepared to sell books out of the trunk of a car.

Equally, I don't believe that people interested in ballet stories are likely to buy them that way.

For the next two years, I tried to get the publisher to send me a royalty statement: even if a book sells not a single copy, the author is entitled to see the statements. In fact, my contract bound the publisher to send me one periodically. However, the truth was that, even though sales might have been slow, there had been some sales, as several people mentioned to me that they had bought it and enjoyed it. So, imagine my surprise when I received a letter one day in 2011, three years after publication (and still not a single royalty statement), informing me that I owed the now-defunct publisher $1,800.00!

The letter was from a woman who revealed the publisher had hired her to wind down operations – this was the first I had heard of the publisher going out of business. She told me that the company owner was ill (it was a small company) and would be retiring, thus freeing the authors from any further obligations to the publisher except for this "unpaid" bill for 100 copies of my book. (How it amounted to that much money, I'll never know. This sum was even higher than retail.) My response was as follows: I most certainly was not going to pay any money for books I did not order—she could have them back if she was prepared to send money for the shipping; nor was I going to pay money to a publisher who had not once provided me with a royalty statement and was therefore in breach of contract. I asked for all rights to revert to me, and I wanted it in writing. That letter came, and not another word was uttered about money owing. I guess threatening to have my lawyer get in touch with them did the trick.

So, there I was with multiple copies of a book that I might as well have published myself from the outset. So, what do you do with a property—a book and its rights—that returns to you?

I decided that the evolution in publishing over the past several years provided me with a significant opportunity to revisit the book and determine whether I could reach a new audience. At this point, the publisher's remnants were unable to provide me with the final, edited manuscript in an editable form, so I used the uneditable version and had it converted. I then began the process of updating the work.

I decided that the book might find an audience these days with the ebook readers, which did not exist when the book was first published. The future was beginning to catch up to me—or I was starting to catch up with the future. I hired a book cover designer to create a more eye-catching cover, and then finished formatting the manuscript for electronic distribution. Then I published it myself via *Kindle Direct* and began letting people know that it was available.

Things had definitely changed in the intervening two to three years in the book-promotion business. With Twitter, Facebook, and other online platforms, within a week I had a request for a review copy from an international dance magazine that evidently had not heard of it before. This was despite my publisher's so-called promotion based on the marketing plan that I had delivered to her at her request.

But what did I learn from all of this that I could use in my future publishing endeavours and that I might share with other unknown writers? Here is what I learned.

- You simply cannot trust your publisher to market your book for you. It's too important. (I already knew this, but the experience brought it into sharp focus.)
- Publishers go out of business and leave you high and dry.
- Authors need to retain some control over their rights, even when signing contracts with traditional publishers.
- If you have a well-edited manuscript (read: professionally edited), you can feel good about indie publishing.

But most importantly, I learned that...

You can breathe new life into old work.

So, as for the future, the dividing line between traditional and indie publishing is getting fuzzier and fuzzier for me. And there are emerging models that are worth considering.

A publishing co-op: An idea whose time has come?

Discussions of traditional publishing versus vanity publishing versus self-publishing always lead to the same conclusion: there has to be a better way in the wake of the new technologies and expectations. And so, the idea of a publishing co-op is born. So, what precisely is a co-op?

There are housing co-ops, banking co-ops, and insurance co-ops. According to the Canadian Co-operative Association, "A co-operative is an organization owned by the members who use its services or are employed there." Further, the association suggests that co-op ventures exist in every part of the economy. So, a bit of research yields some interesting information about terminology in the publishing business.

Some people who have written about cooperative publishing consider it a publishing model representing the middle ground between traditional and print-on-demand publishing. Although this might represent cooperation between an author (who pays) and a "publisher" whom the author contracts, it still says self-publishing to me. The cooperative publishing model I'm suggesting here is based on a business co-op model where, as the CCA says, the business (in this case, the publisher) is owned by the members who use its services. In the case of a *publishing co-op that*

I'm suggesting is worth exploring, the owners both use the services and are the "employees."

The use of the term "co-op" in the publishing business at present clearly does not embrace the ideals of a traditional cooperative business venture. In 2008, one such venture, Ocean Cooperative, charged authors $895 to publish their books; the authors contributed nothing else but the manuscript. This approach is not a cooperative publishing model in any sense of the word. It is a self-publishing model—or at least a supported self-publishing model—since the author is not one of the business owners.

Another venture called BPS was similar. The model that they called a co-op was really not related to what a cooperative business venture is at all. They describe theirs as the model I defined in this book as supported self-publishing. When I refer to the notion of a publishing co-op, I'm suggesting a newer and more exciting approach.

Vala Publishing (now defunct: even co-op publishers can go out of business) had a model closer to the kind I'm working toward here. They described themselves as a community of people who participate in the business of producing books. They called their acquisitions process "grassroots commissioning," a model utilizing people other than editors and marketers, as is the case in the traditional publishing model. The cooperative venture members were the business owners, and their business structure was that of a traditional co-op business venture. However, the members were not necessarily the people who also use the services: some of their members were authors, others involved in the commissioning and acquisitions were not. They set all of this out in a clear business plan. This seemed to be a very interesting and democratic sort of approach to the business of publishing. Still, even that did not quite approach the author-led cooperative publishing business model, where the authors use editorial contractors and make all the decisions on one another's books, which I'm proposing might be worth considering.

Here are some characteristics that I think are worth contemplating in a new publishing model:

- The publishing company is structured like a traditional co-op business venture.
- The owners are the authors.
- The owner/authors all commit to submitting book-length work.
- The owner/authors all commit to participating in the book promotion of their own work and colleagues' work.
- The owner/authors agree on a mission (the kind of work they will and will not publish, size of ownership), vision and values.
- The owner/authors edit one another's work.
- The owner/authors make decisions regarding production issues.
- The owner/authors make decisions regarding distribution contracts.

These features comprise a place to start. There are still many unanswered questions, but it is also exciting to think that innovative approaches are yet to come. The future of the publishing business model has all kinds of possibilities, and authors can reap the benefits.

Future writers in control? Not really

Some years ago, I received an email from a former student who had stumbled upon one of my books online. The book had not been published as an ebook by my publisher, far from it. In fact, when the first edition was published back in 2003, no one was even considering anything but the hold-in-your-hands, paper-between-covers kind of book. However, it was a professional reference handbook that had continued to sell in dribs and drabs, so it was evidently still useful. My student posed this question: *Was I aware that it was available electronically through Questia?* I most assuredly was not.

This experience and what followed with my publisher led me to examine electronic rights and the increasingly odious problem of online literary piracy. Let's use my experiences as the basis for discussing the realities of both of these digital issues, now and in the future.

The electronics rights challenge

Back to the Questia issue. First, what is Questia? It is an online library—a commercial, electronic library with a bit of an academic-type orientation, so your novel isn't likely to end up here, but your nonfiction might, as mine did. According to the best available research, publishers pay a fee to Questia to have their copyrighted material placed on this subscription site. I hold the copyright to the book, and oddly enough, no one consulted me, nor have I ever received any of the "fee" ostensibly paid to my publisher.

I contacted the publisher (a sizeable American textbook publisher that a yet larger American textbook publisher had since acquired) to find out how it got there and why they were not compensating me for its online use. I got precisely nowhere. There was no response to several emails I sent. I was reminded of this when I read a piece by reporter Simon Houpt in the *Globe and Mail* back a few years ago, where he tells the story of the ebook about (God forbid that we should need to know any more about her)

Karla Homolka, accessory to brutal and infamous Canadian rape and murder.

Houpt describes the 14,000-word book *Finding Karla,* which author and journalist Paula Todd decided to release in 2012 as an ebook for a variety of reasons: Todd's primary reason for writing it was that, since she was the one who found Homolka alive and well and living in Guadeloupe, she feared the story might be scooped by other reporters also on her trail. Add to this the idea that a piece of some 14,000 words is more than a magazine feature yet less than a "real" book, and you have a writer seeking a new publishing model and no editor standing in front of you saying that 14,000 words are not enough. Evidently, readers beg to differ.

What's interesting about this story is not the content of Todd's book; rather, it's the story of how publishing models are changing. But Houpt makes an interestingly provocative observation of what might be happening: "…for the first time in decades, some of the power in publishing is shifting back to writers, who are trying to grab the electronic rights that publishers have been taking for granted…"

This issue of who holds power is an ongoing problem with traditional publishers—but they are working on it. These publishers often seem to believe that they have the right to be the sole beneficiaries of the material you slaved over. This belief is one reason why writers consider moving to self-publishing—to retain all rights now and in the future. Of course, these days, a contract is likely to contain a reference to electronic usage, but it still seems that unless we take matters into our own hands, we are the last ones to be paid, rather than the first. The publisher's interest will always come before the writer's interests in traditional publishing contracts. It's just the way it is.

Online literary piracy (& copyright infringement)

It's not a new phenomenon. Writers today just think it is. Literary piracy has been going on since the eighteenth century when British books were reproduced in America without the permission of either the original publisher or the author. The twenty-first century, however, has brought with it new twists to the story.

I was surfing the internet one day when I stumbled upon an online copy of one of my traditionally published books. And I mean, I found a "copy" in the truest sense of the word (not like the electronic Questia copy). The book was there in its entirety, with a cover scan included, and every page posted in a PDF file for all to access. I immediately copied the URL and emailed my publisher in London. The rights editor got back to me very quickly, indicating that they would upload this "piracy" to their "infringement portal" and immediately send a take-down notice.

Unbeknownst to me, my publisher (and presumably others) has access to this "infringement portal" whose purpose is to identify sites like the one I stumbled on. These sites pirate copyrighted material, and they are proliferating as we speak. The site I had inadvertently discovered was new to them and not already identified by their software. The experience spurred me to do some research on the current state of online piracy.

Remember when the music industry clamped down and put Napster out of business? It seems that some of the same activities are happening in the literary world, yet these sites continue to proliferate. Here are the things that I learned from doing a bit of research.

1. Your book may well be pirated. In fact, it likely has already.

2. Even if your book is available only in hard copy, it may still be pirated. Literary pirates can easily procure book-scanning software. The book that I stumbled on is also available as an ebook, but the one I discovered was a scan of the hard copy.
3. There has been an exponential growth in online literary piracy since 2009.
4. Although there is now a well-established anti-literary-piracy movement among publishers, as soon as one site is shut down, another pops up.
5. Piracy sites may have no ethical concerns about stealing your book, but evidently, they are very concerned about being sued. This fear of legal action means that when approached to cease and desist, they usually do so, taking down the identified book.
6. Suppose a traditional publisher publishes you. In that case, they will have an ongoing anti-piracy effort (something you should probably ask them about—I didn't), although some new sites get by them, as in the case where I identified a previously unknown one for my publisher.
7. If you are self-published, you can search for your book regularly or, better yet, set up an ongoing Google search for it. If it pops up on a pirate site, you can prepare and send your own take-down letter by identifying the site's "copyright officer."

It always saddens me that people think there is something different about stealing intellectual property—music, writing, choreography, handbag design—than stealing your cellphone, your car, your wallet. But there is no difference. I like to protect my work, and I hope you think enough of your own work to protect it too.

The end and the beginning

So, we come to the end of our discussions of the myths and realities of writing and publishing in the twenty-first century. As you know by now, I never intended for this book to provide you with instructions for accomplishing your publishing goals. There are so many books on the market today that purport to do that. (*Caveat emptor*.) I wrote it for all those aspiring writers out there, so that you might have someone who has been on this journey for a while to shine a light on some of the myths about writing and publishing and introduce you to some of the realities that face us all. I also wanted to introduce you to ideas and issues that might not have crossed your mind yet, but certainly will if you stay the course on this journey. And it is a journey.

If you truly *are* a writer—not just *someone who wants to have written*—then you will always be on a journey. Each book or article you write and publish will be a milestone along that voyage. Enjoy learning something new with every milestone, and slow down sometimes just to take in the view. This book has been dedicated to you.

Dolly Parton once said, "*I don't like to give advice. I like to give people information because everyone's life is different, and everyone's journey is different.*" I find myself in an unusual position, considering myself a bit like Dolly in this instance. My purpose was to provide you with information—information that I acquired on my own journey. I never intended for this to be advice—to be me saying to you, "Do it this way." You will find a way to do it your own way. But if I can help arm you with information from various perspectives (mine and that of other writers with different stories—different journeys), you will be able to carve your own path. If I have any advice to offer at all, it would be this:

> *Read widely, write a lot, publish only the best.*

I've shared some of the lessons I have learned with you, but there are many more. One day, in the not-too-distant future, you'll probably say, "I wish that damn book had told me this!" In the end, we all have to learn some lessons the hard way.

Before you leave to return to your journals and manuscripts, I'd like to invite you to visit me at www.patriciajparsons.com to share your journey. I'd also invite you to let me know what burning questions you still have. Perhaps I can help you directly and add those topics to future editions of this book.

I wish you well in your new beginning as you finish your book and introduce it to the world. I look forward to reading it.

Before you go…

Be sure to visit me online at www.patriciajparsons.com to see what I'm up to these days.

Then join me on my YouTube channel, **WRITE. FIX. REPEAT.** where I share advice on writing and publishing—five tips at a time.

About the Author

PATRICIA J. PARSONS has been writing professionally since the publication of her first book in 1988 by the now-defunct Toronto publisher NC Press. A nonfiction trade book on the ethics and politics of organ transplantation, that book melded her two backgrounds: health sciences and writing.

Over the years, she's published a variety of works in several different styles, including news and feature writing, trade books, several business books and two text/reference books (one in its third edition/published in the UK), and she has done a substantial amount of corporate writing.

Her book-length works have been published by Doubleday Canada, Wall and Emerson Inc., Dreamcatcher Publishing, and the University of Toronto Press in Canada; Health Administration Press and Routledge in the US; and Kogan Page in the UK. In recent years, she has also made several forays into the world of self-publishing.

Parsons has also explored how her research and nonfiction writing skills could be applied to new genres. She began with memoir writing (published by a small Canadian publisher) and then moved on to historical and women's fiction.

Parsons has also been an accomplished writing teacher for over thirty years. She began teaching writing in the public relations and corporate communications degree program at Mount Saint Vincent University on Canada's east coast, where she has taught news and feature writing as well as corporate writing.

PERMISSION TO WRITE
Sources

Chapter 1

Renee Botcher. Nov. 8, 1999. E-publishing challenges the gatekeeper model. *Infoworld,* 32-33.

Bowker. New Record: More than 1 million books self-published in 2017. http://www.bowker.com/news/2018/New-Record-More-than-1-Million-Books-Self-Published-in-2017.html

Caleb Crain. June 14, 2018. Why we don't read, revisited. *The New Yorker.* https://www.newyorker.com/culture/cultural-comment/why-we-dont-read-revisited

William Zinsser. 1976-2016. *On writing well.* New York: HarperCollins. (many editions since 1976)

Adam Rowe. April 30, 2018. Canadian reading habits say a lot about the future of books. *Forbes* online. https://www.forbes.com/sites/adamrowe1/2018/04/30/canadian-reading-habits-future-books/#3a92ccb6771d

Omar Akkad. May 24, 2014. Digital dilemma: Amazon pushes to package up more profit. *The Globe and Mail.* http://www.theglobeandmail.com/report-on-business/digital-dilemma-amazon-pushes-to-package-up-more-profit/article18831281/

John Boswell. 1986. *The awful truth about publishing: Why they always reject your manuscript and what you can do about it.* New York: Warner Books, p. 3.

Chapter 2

Jenny Diski. October 27, 2006. Want to get rich quick? Don't try writing. *The Guardian Book Blog.* https://www.theguardian.com/books/booksblog/2006/oct/27/wanttogetrichquickdonttr

Chapter 3

Susannah Breslin. June 12, 2012. Why you shouldn't be a writer. *Forbes* online. http://www.forbes.com/sites/susannahbreslin/2012/06/12/why-you-shouldnt-be-a-writer/

Susannah Breslin. March 30, 2013. Why you should be a writer. *Forbes* online. http://www.forbes.com/sites/susannahbreslin/2013/03/30/why-you-should-be-a-writer-2/

Karen Yates. June 23, 2014. 5 reasons you shouldn't write that book. http://goo.gl/S8L05l

Chapter 5

Ben Yagoda. July 22, 2013. Should we write what we know? *The New York Times* online. http://opinionator.blogs.nytimes.com/2013/07/22/should-we-write-what-we-know/?_r=0

Bret Anthony Johnston. July 5, 2011. Don't write what you know. *The Atlantic.*
http://www.theatlantic.com/magazine/archive/2011/08/dont-write-what-you-know/308576/

Hermione Hoby. July 3, 2019. What does it mean to be a "real" writer? *The New Yorker.*
https://www.newyorker.com/books/under-review/what-does-it-mean-to-be-a-real-writer

Chapter 6

William Zinsser. 1976-2016. *On writing well.* New York: HarperCollins. (many editions since 1976)

Chapter 7

Aaron Calvin. January 9, 2014. 16 works that Ernest Hemingway thought a young writer should read: A curated list of must-reads from Papa himself. Buzzfeed.
http://www.buzzfeed.com/aaronc13/16-works-that-ernest-hemingway-thought-a-young-writer-should

Natalie Goldberg. 2005. *Writing down the bones: Freeing the writer within.* Boulder, Colorado: Shambhala Publications.

Anne Mangen and others. October, 2015. Handwriting versus keyboard writing: Effect on word recall. *Journal of Writing Research.* Vol. 7, No. 2.
https://www.researchgate.net/publication/282590558_Handwriting_versus_Keyboard_Writing_Effect_on_Word_Recall

Lee Rourke. November 3, 2011. Why creative writing is better with a pen. *Guardian Book Blog.*

http://www.theguardian.com/books/2011/nov/03/creative-writing-better-pen-longhand

Chapter 9

Chris Baty. 2004. *No plot? No problem*. San Francisco: Chronicle Books, p. 26.

Viki King. 1993. *How to write a movie in 21 days*. San Francisco: Chronicle Books.

Chuck Sambuchino. Word count for novels and children's books: The definitive post. *Writer's Digest*, https://bit.ly/2T9sOaB

K.M. Weiland. January 20, 2010. Why word count goals can be destructive. *Helping Writers Become Authors*. http://www.helpingwritersbecomeauthors.com/2010/01/why-word-count-goals-can-be-destructive.html

Anne Lamott. 1994. *Bird by bird: Some instructions on writing and life*. New York: Doubleday, p. 176-77.

Twyla Tharp. 2003. *The creative habit: Learn it and use it for life*. New York: Simon and Schuster.

The Daily Word Counts of 19 Famous Writers. December 4, 2017. Wordcounter.net. https://wordcounter.net/blog/2017/12/04/103207_the-daily-word-counts-of-19-famous-writers.html

Chapter 10

Catherine Andrews. October 13, 2006. If it's cool, creative and different, it's indie. *CNN.com*. http://www.cnn.com/2006/SHOWBIZ/Music/09/19/indie.overview/

Definition of 'independent.' Oxford English Dictionary online.
https://www.lexico.com/en/definition/independent

Alliance of Independent Authors. Self-Publishing & Independent Authors FAQ.
https://www.allianceindependentauthors.org/independent-indie-author/

Chapter 11

Margaret Shertzer. 1986. *The elements of grammar*. New York: MacMillan Publishing.

William Strunk and E.B. White. 2019. *The elements of style*. 4th ed. New York: MacMillan Publishing. (this is a re-issue. It was originally published in 1959.)

Chapter 12

Brian Klems. August 11, 2016. What is hybrid publishing? Here are 4 things all writers should know. *Writers Digest*.
https://www.writersdigest.com/online-editor/what-is-hybrid-publishing-here-are-4-things-you-should-know

Jeffrey Beall. September 12, 2012. Predatory publishers are corrupting open access. *Nature*.
http://www.nature.com/news/predatory-publishers-are-corrupting-open-access-1.11385

Neil Nixon. 2011. *How to get a break as a writer: Making money from words and ideas*. Troubador Publishing (U.K.), p. 311. See also the archived website Vanity Publishing
http://www.vanitypublishing.info/.

Chapter 13

Mark Medley. 2013. Words from their sponsors: Can authors cash in on crowd-sourced funding sites? *The National Post online* http://arts.nationalpost.com/2013/01/09/words-from-their-sponsors-can-authors-authors-cash-in-on-crowd-sourced-funding-sites/

Unbound. https://unbound.com/about

Chapter 14

Susan Kietzman. December 6, 2017. To publish or pass: The editorial meeting and selecting books for publication. *HuffPost.* https://www.huffpost.com/entry/to-publish-or-to-pass-the_b_4542548

Jenna Glatzer. Why you get form rejection letters. *Writing-world.com.* http://www.writing-world.com/life/form.shtml

Literary Rejections. Bestsellers initially rejected. http://www.litrejections.com/best-sellers-initially-rejected/

Chapter 15

Lev Grossman. January 21, 2009. Books gone wild: The digital age reshapes literature. *Time.* http://content.time.com/time/magazine/article/0,9171,1873122,00.html

Wikipedia. Self-publishing. http://en.wikipedia.org/wiki/Self-publishing

Edward Nawotka. August 18, 2011. Is self-publishing too selfish? *Publishing Perspectives.*

http://publishingperspectives.com/2011/08/is-self-publishing-too-selfish/

Johnathon Clifford. Vanity publishing: A campaign for truth and honesty. (British Library Archived material). http://www.vanitypublishing.info/

Scott Allan. July 24, 2019. How much does it cost to publish a book? A detail of full expenses. *Self-Publishing School*. https://self-publishingschool.com/much-cost-publish-book/

Derek Murphy. June 5, 2018. How much does an average self-publishing author make on Amazon? *Quora Forum*.Fhttps://www.quora.com/How-much-does-an-average-self-publishing-author-make-on-Amazon

Chapter 16

Sarah Juckes. October 4, 2013. How to write an effective blurb for a self-published book. *Alliance of Independent Authors*. http://selfpublishingadvice.org/how-to-write-an-effective-blurb-for-a-self-published-book/

Royale Scuderi. 10 best book recommendation sites you need to know. *Lifehack*. https://www.lifehack.org/articles/technology/10-best-book-recommendation-sites-you-need-know.html

Chapter 17

Jennifer Alsever. April 28, 2014. Guerrilla marketing for books. *CNN Business*. https://money.cnn.com/2014/04/28/smallbusiness/authors-marketing/index.html

B.R. Londhe. 2014. Marketing Mix for Next Generation Marketing. *Procedia Economics and Finance.* Vol. 11, pp. 335-340.

Chapter 18

André Bernard. 1994. *Now all we need is a title: Famous book titles and how they got that way.* New York: W.W. Norton & Company, p. 5.

Terri Giuliano Long. May 30, 2013. Yes, we really do judge books by their covers. *HuffPost.* https://www.huffpost.com/entry/book-cover-design-indies_n_3354504

Writers Digest Online. October 3, 2018. The anatomy of a book cover: A guide for authors. https://www.writersdigest.com/editor-blogs/there-are-no-rules/marketing-self-promotion/the-anatomy-of-a-book-cover-a-guide-for-authors

Tim Kreider. July 16, 2013. The decline and fall of the book cover. *The New Yorker* online. http://www.newyorker.com/online/blogs/books/2013/07/the-decline-and-fall-of-the-book-cover.html

Writer's Digest. February 17, 2011. 10 tips for effective book covers. *Writer's Digest.* http://www.writersdigest.com/editor-blogs/there-are-no-rules/general/10-tips-for-effective-book-covers

Chapter 19

Paul Hiebert. September 15, 2010. Against promotional author photographs. *Flavorwire.*

http://flavorwire.com/117566/against-promotional-author-photographs

David Wills. December 7, 2011. Curse of the douchey author photo. *TNB*. http://www.thenervousbreakdown.com/dswills/2011/12/curse-of-the-douchey-author-photo/

Noah Charney. October 17, 2015. The not-quite end of the book tour. *The Atlantic*. https://www.theatlantic.com/entertainment/archive/2015/10/the-modern-face-of-book-tours/407641/

Douglas Bell. October 15, 2011. The season of readings is upon us: Let the misery begin. *The Globe and Mail*. http://www.theglobeandmail.com/news/arts/books/the-season-of-readings-is-upon-us-let-the-misery-begin/article2201498/

David Streitfield. August 25, 2012. The best book reviews money can buy. *The New York Times* online. http://goo.gl/YcZDvA

Ashlee Kieler. September 4, 2015. Amazon files first lawsuit to block companies from selling fraudulent positive reviews. *Consumerist*. https://consumerist.com/2015/04/09/amazon-files-first-lawsuit-to-block-companies-from-selling-fraudulent-positive-reviews/

Science Fiction and Fantasy Writers of America. August 12, 2009. Contest and award fakes. https://www.sfwa.org/other-resources/for-authors/writer-beware/contests/

Chapter 20

Carly Watters. September 9, 2013. 6 ways social media doesn't help you get published. https://carlywatters.com/2013/09/09/6-ways-social-media-doesnt-help-you-get-published/

Jane Friedman. August 16, 2011. 3 principles for Facebook fan pages. http://janefriedman.com/2011/08/16/3-principles-facebook-fan-pages/

David Henry Sterry. May 25, 2011. Does an author really need a website? *Huffington Post online*. http://www.huffingtonpost.com/david-henry-sterry/does-an-author-really-nee_b_820562.html

Jane Friedman. November 13, 2017. Unpublished writers and websites: Should you have one and what should it say? https://www.janefriedman.com/unpublished-writers-websites/

Anne Allen. 7 ways authors waste time building 'platform' on social media. http://annerallen.blogspot.ca/2013/06/7-ways-authors-waste-time-building.html

Fauzia Burke. April 9, 2013. Does social media sell books? http://www.huffingtonpost.com/fauzia-burke/book-sales-social-media_b_2616439.html

Rob Eager. March 23, 2016. Does social media marketing actually sell books? *Book Business*. https://www.bookbusinessmag.com/post/social-media-marketing-actually-sell-books/

Gabriel Pena i Ballesté and others. January 19, 2014. Book trailers serve as a multiplier for book discovery. *Publishing Perspectives*.

http://publishingperspectives.com/2014/01/book-trailers-serve-as-a-multiplier-for-book-discovery/

Chapter 21

Canadian Cooperative Association.

    http://www.coopscanada.coop/en/about_co-operative/about_co-ops

Simon Houpt. April 30, 2018 (updated). Does a $3 e-book on Karla Homolka represent a new wave of journalism? *The Globe and Mail*. http://goo.gl/JSYLO6

www.gendocs.ru

www.ingramcontent.com/pod-product-compliance
Lightning Source LLC
Chambersburg PA
CBHW031947080426
42735CB00007B/298